David Morrison

The American River

DELTA Publishing

You can listen to the audio clues for *The American River* using the free
DELTA Augmented app – you'll also find fun interactive activities!

Download the free DELTA Augmented app onto your device	Start picture recognition and scan the **contents page**	Download files and use them now or save them for later

Apple and the Apple logo are trademarks of Apple Inc., registered in the US and other
countries. App Store is a service mark of Apple Inc. | Google Play and the Google Play logo
are trademarks of Google Inc.

1st edition   1 5 4 3 2 1 | 2027 26 25 24 23

Delta Publishing, 2023
www.deltapublishing.co.uk

© Ernst Klett Sprachen GmbH, Rotebühlstraße 77, 70178 Stuttgart, 2023

Author: David Morrison
Editor: Kate Baade
Concept: Kate Baade, David Morrison

Cover and layout: Eva Lettenmayer
Illustrations: Peter Nagy, Beehive Illustration
Cover picture: Peter Nagy, Beehive Illustration
Design: Datagroup Int. SRL, Timisoara, Romania
Printing and binding: Plump Druck & Medien GmbH, Rheinbreitbach

ISBN 978-3-12-501154-0

Contents

About this book...5

Read, think, and solve the enigma to find the number of the first page of the next chapter

Sunday history trips..?
You're a smart kid, AD ....?
Murrieta's real hideaway..?
It all goes back to the river ....?
Seeing the elephant..?
A time tunnel...?
Sleepyhead ....?
Fishhooks...?
For want of a nail ....?
Shot like a dog, by a dog ....?
Hocus pocus...?
Pinyin..?

Build your vocabulary...149
Find out more...154
Answer key..156

Abbreviations

sth = something
sb = somebody

About this book

This is you.

You're the main character in this book.

In fact, you *wrote* it and you'll live in its pages until you manage to escape from them …

How? By solving the enigmas at the end of each chapter, which will give you the number of the first page of the next chapter you need to read.

Eventually, everything will make sense and you'll escape, having relived the adventure you had on your thirteenth birthday, in an abandoned hotel in a deserted 1850's Californian Gold Rush town, called Miner's Haven, right by the majestic American River.

Along the way, you'll encounter a range of curious characters, including a bandit, a bounty hunter, a native American guide, circus performers, an assayer, a botanist, a photographer, and a murdered man.

So, just how do you escape?

Follow these guidelines:
- Make sure you read the introduction to each chapter. This will energize your mind for the challenge ahead.
- Pay close attention to everything you read and see. There are clues everywhere!
- At the end of each chapter, you need to find a number. This number is the number of the first page of the next chapter you need to read. Your goal is to reach the last chapter and finish the book.
- Read the fact files. These will give you background information about the Californian Gold Rush and the people who experienced it. This information could be useful.

- You could cheat, of course, but this book will let everybody else who reads or is reading it know that you've done so; and that would just be really embarrassing, right?
- That said, if you do need some help, listen to the downloadable clue when indicated.
- A bookmark, notebook and pencil will be very useful!

Finding your way out of an Escape Adventure in English is a real achievement! So, when you do get out, make sure you celebrate the fact (before you choose another title from the DELTA Escape Adventure series to read, of course)!

Good luck! You'll need it 😉 … And remember, it all comes back to the river, AD … The American River.

Names and ideas

Here are some of the people and events you will encounter along the way. What do you know about them? Use the internet to find out more and make notes.

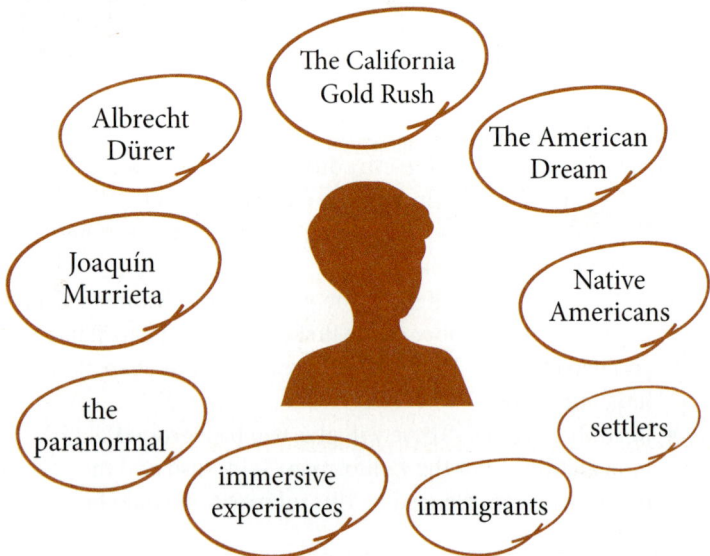

The California Gold Rush

Albrecht Dürer

The American Dream

Joaquín Murrieta

Native Americans

the paranormal

settlers

immersive experiences

immigrants

Sunday history trips

When you've escaped this chapter, check your answers to these questions by looking at the answer key on page 156.

Main characters

Match the main characters in this chapter to their descriptions.

AD	your twin brothers
Selena Dresler	you
Rosa Murrieta Dresler	your sister
Jake and Elmore Dresler	your mom
Karl Dresler	your dad

What do you think this is?

Test your general knowledge

Choose an answer for each of the questions below.

1. The California Gold Rush started in:
    a. the 1890s
    b. the 1850s
    c. the 1840s

2. In modern day Northern California the main industry is:
   a. fishing
   b. electronic technology
   c. oil

3. During the Californian Gold Rush, Joaquín Murrieta was a famous:
   a. bandit
   b. minerologist
   c. doctor

Useful words and expressions

Knowing the meaning of these words will help you escape from this chapter.

A haven is a place that protects people.

To strike it rich is to suddenly have lots of money.

Nuggets are pieces of gold in its natural state.

A combination lock is a device to close, for example, doors. The correct number combination opens the device.

Talking point

One of the characters in this chapter says, "Ghosts are for losers". What do you think about the paranormal? Talk to your classmates, friends or family and share your ideas and experiences.

You don't want to be here.

It's May 13, your birthday, and you'd rather be in Sacramento visiting the Crocker Art Museum, taking yet another close-up look at the Albrecht Dürer drawing the museum owns (and that you love), "Female Nude with a Staff," or sitting in the sunshine in McKinley Park, reading a book or drawing in your sketchbook, and signing each drawing with your version of the cool monogram Albrecht Dürer himself signed his creations with, then sending your drawings, by cellphone message, to your best friend, George.

But you're doing none of those things.

Just like every Sunday, you're pretending, and not very successfully, to be interested in your mom and dad's passion for the Gold Rush and the success stories they just *love* discovering about people like your German and Mexican ancestors, who

---

25 **monogram** symbol made by combining letters – 29 **to pretend** to make it look as though – 32 **ancestor** sb in your family or from your country who lived before your time

overcame all sorts of difficulties to make their fortune and help found modern-day California, "where anything is possible."

You haven't told them this, of course, but as far as you can see, your mom and dad don't seem a tiny bit interested in finding out about the hundreds of thousands of people who ruined their health and bankrupted their families by coming to California by land and sea, in search of gold.

But hey, "Think positive, be positive and positive things will happen!," your dad always says, before he half-sings, half-says the new mantra both he and your mom just LOVE: *"Yəti'iškom malawa"* which, you suppose, means something profound in Japanese.

Sundays are always like this.

Your mom and dad come up with a mad plan over breakfast and your younger twin brothers Jake and Elwood and your sister Selena get excited about it.

Then off you go (sometimes, in your case, like a stick of 49ers' dynamite, at least inside) in the turquoise 1960s camper van your dad bought last year then paid to have restored (Jake and Elwood say the big, chrome badge on the front of the camper van means "Very Wowza," which is quite funny, you suppose).

You don't actually *hate* your family, of course, you just want a bit more space. Your mom, Rosa, who's thirty-eight, and your dad, Karl, who's thirty-seven, are both *super-smart*. They own a deeply cool and very successful interactive technology company, called Murriet@, in Los Gatos, the town where you live. Murriet@ has some of the biggest names in Silicon Valley as its clients and your mom and dad both teach a User Experience course at the San José State University, too. And

---

1 **to overcome** to deal successfully with sth – 11 **profound** deep and meaningful

your mom is always ready to help friends, family and neighbors with her herbal medicine remedies (which actually work, sometimes).

Even Jake and Elwood and Selena (okay, even Jake and Elwood) are fun to be with, sometimes.

Just not *this* Sunday.

For a few months now, it's felt like an enormous challenge to take part in these "educational-but-fun" Sunday history trips and today, especially, your birthday, you're really finding it difficult to hide your boredom.

Maybe it's because you're still a little young to take interest in the adult things your parents talk about. Maybe it's because you're *much* too old to really enjoy Jake and Elwood's silly games.

As for Selena ("our little moonchild," as your mom and dad call her because she was born on a night when there was a full moon), she just irritates you, *full stop, almost all the time.* I mean, how can anyone so young (she's only ten) be *so* materialistic?

No, you're definitely *not* looking forward to visiting Miner's Haven, a *fascinating* (according to your dad), tiny, abandoned Gold Rush mining village by The American River, North Fork.

Besides, it's taking ages to get there because you made a long stop along the way at a rest area just off Interstate 80, so Jake and Elmore could use the bathroom (it always amazes you that they both need to go at the same time) and so that Selena could buy something (or anything), which is her favorite thing in the world to do, and it took her *ages* to choose an Interstate 80 fridge magnet, of all things.

Your dad looks at you in the rearview mirror.

"Remember that gold rush project you did in second grade, AD?"

Your parents have called you "AD" for as long as you can remember. You don't mind. Other people call you that, too. Almost everyone does, in fact. You like to think that maybe people called Albrecht Dürer that too, back in the day, only with a German accent: "ah, day."

"Yeah, Dad," you answer, as patiently as you can.

Then your mom asks: "Anything you learned doing the project that you'd like to share with us, AD?"

You conquer your desire to answer her question with a rude "nope" and, like the good sibling you are, explain to Jake, Elmore and Selena that lots of people came to Northern California at the end of 1848 and more in 1849 and in the 1850s from all over the world, to try to make their fortune by finding gold along The American River.

DID YOU KNOW?

10 FUN FACTS ABOUT
THE CALIFORNIAN GOLDRUSH

Fact 1: There were hardly any female 49ers in California during the Gold Rush. In 1852, only 8 percent of California's immigrant population were women. In 1860, the percentage of women in the immigrant population was still only 19%.

Fact 2: The ships bringing gold miners to California were used as construction material. Houses, banks, saloons, hotels, jails and other structures were built using wood and other objects from the ships that gold miners abandoned as soon as they arrived in San Francisco.

Fact 3: Everything was expensive during the Californian Gold Rush. In today's money, in 1849 miners could pay $25 for an egg and $2,500 for a new pair of leather boots!

---

6 **to conquer your desire to** to manage not to

Fact 4: Many commercial empires were born during the California Gold Rush. A good example is that of Levi Strauss, a Bavarian who arrived in San Francisco in 1850 with plans to open a shop selling tents and wagon coverings. Quickly, Strauss began making strong trousers out of denim and very soon he had made his fortune!

Fact 5: Two brothers mined $1.5 million worth of gold in a single year. John and Daniel Murphy arrived in the Sierra Nevada in 1848 and struck gold within days. In a year, they mined $1.5 million worth of gold, which, at today's prices is the equivalent of $40 million!

Fact 6: San Francisco became a city in two years. At the start of the gold rush, the population of San Francisco, a small port on the Pacific Ocean was 1,000. In 1850, it was 20,000. And in 1861, 56,000!

Fact 7: If you got rich, you ordered a Hangtown Fry. Named after a violent mining town, this mixture of eggs and bacon fat omelette and fried oysters became the traditional miners' celebration food when they found gold. You can still order it today in many restaurants in San Francisco.

Fact 8: Gold has been around for a long, long time. Gold has been discovered on every continent on Earth and has been mined for over 5,000 years. Experts estimate that humans have mined 142,000 metric tons of gold in total.

Fact 9: Gold is a strange mineral. The physical and chemical properties of gold mean:
- it does not oxidize;
- it conducts heat and electricity;
- it can be made into thread;
- it is edible;
- it is chemically inactive.

Fact 10: Our bodies contain gold. Human bones contain 0.016 parts per million of gold and the average adult human body contains 0.2 mg.

"Hardly any of them made any money, though," you explain. "Actually, most of the people who came either went home poor or started doing something else. I mean it was almost impossible to survive if you didn't have lots of money or strike it rich, which only a few people did, because the price of everything was so high."

"That's terrible," says Selena. "How can anyone enjoy life if they can't buy stuff?"

You pretend you haven't heard your sister and say, "And the Gold Rush was deadly for anyone from one of the indigenous tribes who lived around here, too. Most of them were killed by the gold diggers who made them slaves or by the diseases they brought with them."

At this point, your dad gives your mom a look you can't interpret.

Then he says, "Well remembered, AD! As far as making it rich goes, you're right. For many settlers, owning a shop became the real dream."

"Yep," agrees your mom. "Folk used to say that it was easier to mine the miner than mine the land!"

"And nothing's changed, Rosa, has it?" says your dad, with a knowing smile.

Then nobody says anything, and your dad tunes the radio to Classic Soul FM and he and your mom begin singing along to Aretha Franklin.

Following the instructions that the camper van's GPS device has just given him, your dad turns off the main road onto another narrow dirt track along a valley between two mountains.

---

9 **indigenous** native to a country. In this adventure you will see the terms Native Indian and Native American. We use the term Native Indian when referring to the time of the Gold Rush, and Native American when referring to more recent times. – 10 **tribe** group of people from a shared community

And after driving for about a mile, you arrive in Miner's Haven.

"Cool!" says Jake, as you come to a stop next to a sign with some of its metal letters missing, so that it says "MIN   A."

"*Très, très* cool!" says Elwood.

You remove your cellphone from the cable connecting it to one of the USB charger ports your dad had installed during the renovation of the camper van and you message your friend George:

> Here, at last. Empty wooden buildings, shrubs and dirt.😕 Yippee! Bye for now!

Your dad parks the camper van and you all get out.

Even though it's not *so* hot yet, the sound of crickets fills the air.

In the distance you can see abandoned wooden buildings with tin roofs and collapsed porches and one or two houses made with adobe and missing their roofs.

"Dad, there's nothing here," says Selena.

Your dad locks the van doors and replies: "Maybe there's nothing that immediately meets the eye; but this place must be *full* of stories. We just have to find them, that's all. It's a ghost town, Selena."

"Ghosts are for losers," replies Selena, bad-temperedly.

"Miner's Haven was an amazing place, once, Selena," your dad replies. "Apparently, the nuggets miners found here were 99,95% gold! Who knows, we might find some treasure of our own!"

"Wowza!" shout Jake and Elwood, who then run off towards a rusty windmill that presumably once powered a water pump, next to a wooden building with no roof, near a cemetery where there are a dozen graves consisting of wooden crosses and lines of stone over the bodies below.

The twins climb up the iron structure that keeps the water pump windmill in the air.

---

4 **très** very *(French)* – 9 **shrub** small bush – 17 **adobe** a kind of clay used for building – 22 **bad-temperedly** in a bad mood – 27 **presumably** probably

"Get down right now!" shouts your mom.

"Jake, Elwood, come see!" shouts your dad as he takes a piece of paper from one of the thigh pockets of his cargo pants.

Your twin brothers sprint back and your dad kneels on the gray ground and unfolds the paper to reveal a map of Miner's Haven.

"Good thinking, Karl," says your mom.

"Yeah, I found a photograph of it yesterday, on the El Dorado County Public Library's web site, so I drew a copy."

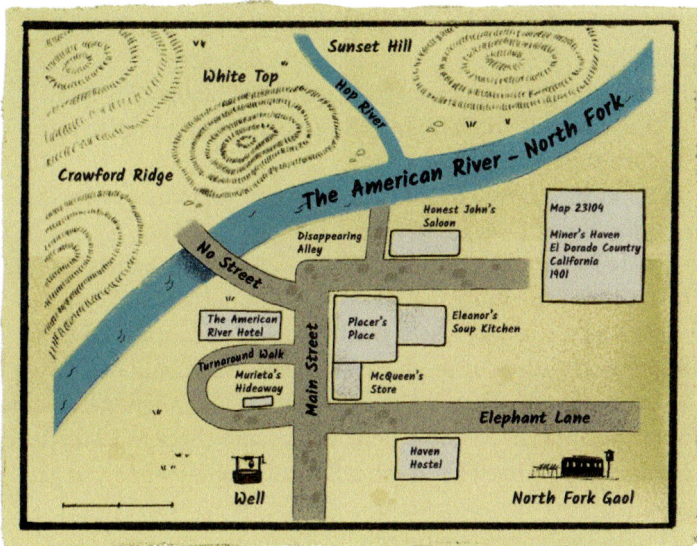

Your dad stands up again and hands the map to your mom.

"Actually, I drew five copies, so we all have one."

Your dad gives you and your brothers and sister a map each. You wonder why he didn't just print the photograph of the map, but you say nothing: after all, how many fun treasure maps has he drawn for you, Selena, Jake and Elwood over the years?

---

5 **to reveal** to show

The map shows that Miner's Haven is surrounded by three mountains: White Top, Crawford Ridge and Sunset Hill. Nothing unusual about those names, you think.

The five street names on the map, however, *are* unusual: Disappearing Alley, No Street, Elephant Lane, Placer's Place, Main Street and Turnaround Walk.

The names written next to the six buildings on the map are: Honest John's Saloon, Haven Hostel, The American River Hotel, Eleanor's Soup Kitchen, McQueen's Store and North Fork Gaol.

"Look, here it says Murrieta's Hideaway, Dad," says Jake, excitedly.

"Murrieta, Dad! Just like Mom's surname!" shouts Elwood.

"Very wowza!" shouts Jake as he gives Elwood a high five.

Selena yawns.

Your mom turns to look at you and says, "AD knows who *the* Joaquín Murrieta, was, don't you AD?"

Selena stares at you with a face that says she just knows you are about to say something *really* boring, or stupid, or both.

Then, unexpectedly (he normally wants you to stick close to and interact with your brothers and sister, even if you don't want to), your dad says, "You know what? I think AD might need some *alone time*. In fact, AD, why don't you go and check out Murrieta's Hideaway by yourself? You can tell us all about it when you get back."

"O-kay," you reply, confusedly.

"Back from outer space …," mumbles Selena, who receives a stern look from your mom.

"You've got your cellphone, right, AD?" asks your mom.

You nod and reluctantly walk off down Main Street.

After a few yards, you turn left into Turnaround Walk, the gray dust track next to which Murrieta's Hideaway still stands: a tiny,

---

26 **to mumble** to speak unclearly – 27 **stern** serious – 29 **reluctantly** not wanting to

18

one-floor shack. You take a
photo of the shack.

You go inside and discover
a living room, kitchen, and
bedroom. In all of these
rooms, the floor is covered with gray
dust from the "road" outside.

In the living room, there's a table big enough for one
person to eat at. On the table, there's an oil lamp, a clay pipe
and an old, unopened letter, addressed, simply, to J.M., Miner's
Haven, El Dorado, California. There is no stamp.

You pick up the letter and go into the other room in the house,
a bedroom, where, in the corner of the room, there's a rusty
wood burner.

You fold your dad's map and put it into one of the back pockets
of your pants. You put the unopened letter in the other.

Then, with your cellphone, you record a video of Murrieta's
Hideaway and send the video to George.

A reply comes quickly.

You notice that your battery charge has suddenly gone down
from 99% to 30%.

Like it! 😊 Who lived there?

Well, it's called Murrieta's Hideaway …

You're kidding me! *The* Joaquín Murrieta?
The Mexican Robin Hood you pretend your mom's
descended from? Wow! 😉

---

1 **shack** a small wooden building – 32 **to be descended from** to be directly related to

Suppose so …

So what's in the wardrobe? 😌
Happy Birthday, by the way!

You go back into the bedroom. The wardrobe reminds you of one of the books you and George read last year, at the same time, *The Lion, the Witch and the Wardrobe*, by C.S. Lewis.

Then you notice that the wardrobe's doors are held closed by a small, two-digit combination lock, far newer than anything else in the house. In fact, it's brand new!

You try random combinations to open the lock but have no success, so you write a message to George and send it to her with a photo of the locked wardrobe doors.

Any ideas?

You wait for a minute but get no reply, so you decide to search the shack for a clue. As far as you can see, however, there's nothing to help you, so you go outside again, step off the porch and walk round to the back of the shack.

From there you can see your family's camper van, parked in the same place as before, but you can't see your family anywhere. They're probably exploring some other old wooden box of a building, you assume.

---

14 **brand new** completely new – 27 **porch** terrace in front of a house

---

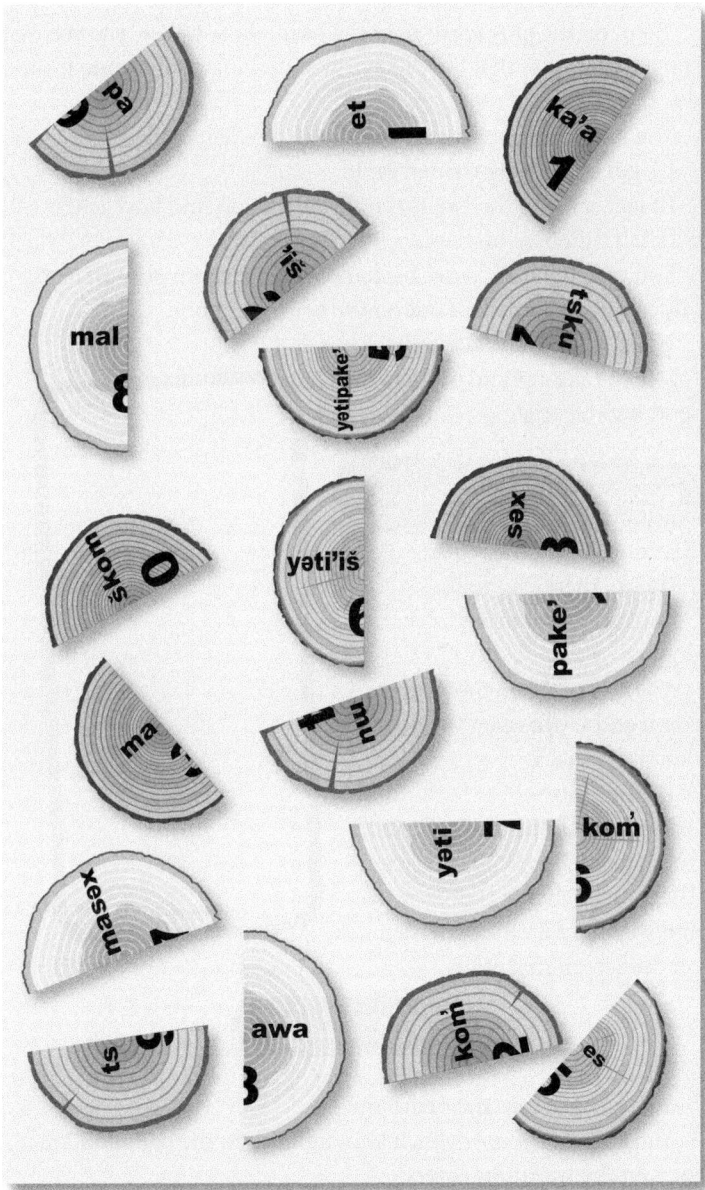

Then, on the gray earth near the back of the house, you see some half-circles that look like broken biscuits, only made from wood.

You kneel down and turn one of the wooden circle halves over.

It's got something written on it.

In fact, each of the twenty circle halves you find have letters and half numbers on them.

You take the half circles back into the bedroom of Murrieta's Hideaway and lay them out on the bedroom floor.

Next, you put the circles back together, take a photo of them and send it to George.

> Any idea what language this is?

Word	Number
	,

Again, there's no reply.

Suddenly, you hear the shack door close.

You go back into the living room and try to open the door out of the shack.

It won't move.

Your cellphone starts to buzz. You take it out of your pocket. The battery charge is now at 5% and there is a flashing message on the screen that reads

> DANGER!

You go back into the bedroom.

You still don't know which two digits open the combination lock on the wardrobe doors.

You think hard.

Yes! That's it! That thing that both Mom and Dad have been chanting non-stop recently. Their "mantra." You're sure there were words from the number circles in it …

You look at the circles and see that the two words in your parents' "mantra" correspond to two numbers on the wooden circles. You try the numbers on the combination lock and it opens.

Listen to the clue!

Now turn to page _____.

You're a smart kid, AD

When you've escaped this chapter, check your answers to these questions by looking at the answer key on page 156.

Main character

The main character in this chapter is Jean-Pierre Aurelian, the assayer in Miner's Haven. Which of these facts about Jean-Pierre Aurelian do you think are true? Tick.

He had a French accent.	
He had a beard.	
His office was in The American River Hotel.	
He was a chemist.	
He was poorly dressed.	

Do you know what this is?

Test your general knowledge

Choose an answer for each of the questions below.

1. At first, what did gold miners use to extract gold from Californian rivers?
   a. magnets
   b. pans
   c. boats

2. The name of a piece of gold in the shape of a rectangle and often stored in banks is:
   a. an ingot
   b. a stone
   c. a goldilock

3. During the Californian Gold Rush, lots of money was made by:
   a. everybody
   b. people who owned mining equipment shops
   c. nobody

Useful words and expressions

Knowing the meaning of these words will help you escape from this chapter.

An assayer is a chemist specialized in calculating the weight and quality of gold.

A newcomer is somebody who has just arrived at a place for the first time.

To stare is to look at something or someone directly for a long time.

Scales are an instrument that show us the weight of an object or objects.

Talking point

The main character in this chapter explains to AD that in 1846, there were only 8,000 non-Indian Native people in California, but by 1860, there were 380,000, 98% of whom were men. What are the the main reasons people migrate or emigrate? Talk to your classmates, friends or family and share your ideas and experiences.

You go straight to door 24.
You enter the room.

Instead of shutters, there are curtains at the window and these
are open. There is no glass in the window and metal bars run
from top to bottom and from right to left on the outside. There is
no bed and no chairs and the walls are bare except for a periodic
chart on the chimney breast and a chemistry laboratory had been
installed in the room. The door into the room has, of course,
closed. To the right of it hangs a shotgun.

"Well done for making it this far, AD."

The voice is coming from outside the window.

You approach the window and see a bearded man wearing a
top hat, standing two or three meters away.

He looks a bit like Abraham Lincoln and has a French accent.

21 **shutter** wooden panel you can move across a window to make a room dark
25 **chimney breast** the part of a chimney directly above a fireplace

"Jean-Pierre Aurelian at your service. I was the assayer around here from 1851 to 1857. That's my office you're standing in, right there, in The American River Hotel, where most of your ancestors once stayed, though later the winds of life blew them to different corners of the Federation, and the world, including *me*.

"Because the Gold Rush was quite something, AD! Take the man who told the world about the gold found near Coloma, Old Sam Brannan. In nine weeks in 1849, he made 36,000 dollars by selling supplies to miners. That's the equivalent of more than 750,000 dollars today. He sold the pans the miners needed to find the gold in the river mud for 15 dollars each when he'd bought them for 15 cents. Or just the amount of people who came here from around the world. In 1846, there were only 8,000 non-Indian Native people in California. By 1860, there were 380,000, 98% of whom were men. In the same period, the Indian population fell from 150,000 to 30,000. And just look at the Chinese. In 1848, there were 7 Chinese men in California and in 1860 there were about 12,000 Chinese people, and only 11 of them were adult women.

"And the money made was incredible, AD. From 1849 to 1852, gold worth more than 2,000,000,000 dollars, in today's money, was extracted from the gold fields!

"But enough of boring facts, AD. Time is of the essence. You still have to find the treasure and your battery's running low again."

"The treasure?" you ask.

"Yes, the treasure, AD. You'll need the map that's hidden in the shotgun barrel. Take it with you before you leave my office. But how do you leave, AD, that's the question, isn't it?

"Yeah, that and what will happen when my battery charge hits zero. And what are all the tragedies going on upstairs.

"Oh, don't worry about the tragedies, AD. All the best families have them. And you're too smart for your battery to hit zero, trust me. Let me tell you about my profession, then I'll help you. Back then, the first step in turning gold into money was for a man like me, a trained chemist, to weigh and assay it. Once I'd been given the nuggets of gold by miners, I melted them in a furnace, that's the thing next to the fire, and then poured the molten gold into an iron mold to form a bar called an ingot.

"I let the ingot cool and then I cut two small pieces from opposite corners of it. I did chemical analysis on one of these pieces to determine its purity. The other piece was my commission. So, the more gold folk found, the more I worked, and the richer I got.

"And we did get rich, AD, the assayers. It was my money, for example, not James Thomas' or his family's (and certainly not his mother's, God forbid), that built this hotel. Seven rooms for guests who actually lived here, as I did, downstairs; ten rooms for newcomers or passing visitors upstairs, a lobby, a kitchen, a dining room and a library. I insisted there was a library before investing in James Thomas' idea. And I was happy here for a good few years, AD. James and Mona ran the hotel well and I enjoyed the company of Joaquín and Gabriela Murrieta and their daughter, Aurora; Uwe Dresler, Pin and Yin, Robert White, a good man who made a fatal mistake, and Saul Gregson, who ended up marrying Sarah Thomas, James Thomas' mother.

"But back to the gold. The last step in the process was to stamp the ingot with my professional information. Then I gave the gold back to its owner with a certificate stating it's providence, weight, and purity, and I received my fee.

"Now, there's a periodic table on the wall, AD. You need to find a word. Then you need to add the numbers that correspond to the chemical symbols that make up the word, AD. It's simple for a smart kid like you."

---

3 **nugget** piece (of gold) – 5 **ingot** bar of gold – 27 **fee** payment

You turn round to look at the periodic table.

"For example, imagine the word was "lace". In that case, you'd need the symbols for lanthanum, La, and cerium, Ce. All the symbols have a number, their atomic number. For "LaCe" you'd add 57 and 58 to get 115.

"Oh, and then you need to subtract 198 from the result of your addition and put the resulting number, in ounces on the scales. And you can't use carbon. Got it, AD?"

You see the scales the assayer is talking about in a corner of the room.

"Any questions, AD?"

You turn back to the window and say: "But which word?"

"The river, AD. It all comes back to the river."

"What?"

"You're a smart kid, AD. The river …"

And then he is gone.

You walk towards the periodic table and stare at it as if it was incomprehensible, just like you do every week in chemistry class.

---

10 **ounce** imperial measurement (1 ounce = 28g) – 10 **scales** device used to weigh materials – 21 **incomprehensible** impossible to understand

DID YOU KNOW?

10 FUN FACTS ABOUT THE PERIODIC TABLE

(H) **Fact 1: The periodic table was inspired by a dream.**
The inventor of the definitive periodic table, the Russian scientist Dmitri Mendeleev, said, "I saw in a dream a table where all elements fell into place as required. Awakening, I immediately wrote it down on a piece of paper, only in one place did a correction later seem necessary."

(Au) **Fact 2: Mendeleev was a visionary.**
In 1869, because all the elements were not known, there were spaces on Mendeleev's table. However, Mendeleev predicted the properties of some of the missing elements.

(Mg) **Fact 3: Mendeleev loved playing the card game Solitaire.**
This partly explains the distribution of the periodic table.

(Na) **Fact 4: Science has honoured Mendeleev.**
A large crater on the far side of the Moon is named after Mendeleev.

(O) **Fact 5: The building bricks of our universe are contained in the periodic table.**
The elements in the periodic tables cannot be separated into simpler substances by any chemical reaction.

(Al) **Fact 6: There really are a lot of elements!**
Scientists have identified 118 chemical elements. However, approximately 20 percent of these do not exist in nature (or are present only in trace amounts). We know about them because they have been synthetically produced in the laboratory.

(Fe) **Fact 7: The periodic table is updated, periodically.**
For example, four new elements were added in 2016.

(Ts) **Fact 8: All elements need a name.**
The latest elements to be discovered are called: Nihonium
(Nh), Moscovium (Mc), Tennessine (Ts), and Oganesson
(Og).

(Ag) **Fact 9: Heavy metal!**
About 75 percent of the periodic table is composed of metals.

(Ge) **Fact 10: Where do the names of elements come from?**
There are many inspirations for the names of elements.
Einsteinium is named after Albert Einstein. Germanium,
Americium, and Gallium were named after the countries
where they were discovered. Thorium is named after the
Scandinavian god of thunder, Thor, and Titanium after
the Ancient Greek Titans.

"The river," you say to yourself. "It all goes back to the river."
You look for element symbols that make up the word "river"
but get nowhere.

Was Jean-Pierre Aurelian talking about The *American* River?
You make the word "American" using symbols for five
elements, none of which is carbon.

You add up the corresponding atomic numbers and get _____.
Then you subtract 198 from that number.

Listen to the clue!

Finally, you walk over to the assayer's scales, put _____ ounces
on them and hear a familiar click: the door into the room has just
opened.

You take the shotgun down and remove the map that's rolled
up inside its barrel.

Then you run into the corridor, looking for door _____.

PERIODIC TABLE OF THE ELEMENTS

Legend (key): Atomic number — 5 · Atomic mass 10.811 · Symbol **B** · Name BORON

Categories: Alkali metal · Alkaline earth metal · Metal · Transition metal · Lanthanide · Metalloid · Non-metal · Halogen · Noble gas · Actinide

Z	Symbol	Name	Atomic mass
1	H	Hydrogen	1.0079
2	He	Helium	4.0026
3	Li	Lithium	6.941
4	Be	Beryllium	9.0122
5	B	Boron	10.811
6	C	Carbon	12.011
7	N	Nitrogen	14.007
8	O	Oxygen	15.999
9	F	Fluorine	18.998
10	Ne	Neon	20.180
11	Na	Sodium	22.990
12	Mg	Magnesium	24.305
13	Al	Aluminium	26.982
14	Si	Silicon	28.086
15	P	Phosphorus	30.974
16	S	Sulfur	32.065
17	Cl	Chlorine	35.453
18	Ar	Argon	39.948
19	K	Potassium	39.098
20	Ca	Calcium	40.078
21	Sc	Scandium	44.956
22	Ti	Titanium	47.867
23	V	Vanadium	50.942
24	Cr	Chromium	51.996
25	Mn	Manganese	54.938
26	Fe	Iron	55.845
27	Co	Cobalt	58.933
28	Ni	Nickel	58.693
29	Cu	Copper	63.546
30	Zn	Zinc	65.38
31	Ga	Gallium	69.723
32	Ge	Germanium	72.64
33	As	Arsenic	74.922
34	Se	Selenium	78.96
35	Br	Bromine	79.904
36	Kr	Krypton	83.798
37	Rb	Rubidium	85.468
38	Sr	Strontium	87.62
39	Y	Yttrium	88.906
40	Zr	Zirconium	91.224
41	Nb	Niobium	92.906
42	Mo	Molybdenum	95.96
43	Tc	Technetium	(98)
44	Ru	Ruthenium	101.07
45	Rh	Rhodium	102.91
46	Pd	Palladium	106.42
47	Ag	Silver	107.87
48	Cd	Cadmium	112.41
49	In	Indium	114.82
50	Sn	Tin	118.71
51	Sb	Antimony	121.76
52	Te	Tellurium	127.60
53	I	Iodine	126.90
54	Xe	Xenon	131.29
55	Cs	Caesium	132.91
56	Ba	Barium	137.33
57 – 71	La-Lu	Lanthanide	
72	Hf	Hafnium	178.49
73	Ta	Tantalum	180.95
74	W	Tungsten	183.84
75	Re	Rhenium	186.21
76	Os	Osmium	190.23
77	Ir	Iridium	192.22
78	Pt	Platinum	195.08
79	Au	Gold	196.97
80	Hg	Mercury	200.59
81	Tl	Thallium	204.38
82	Pb	Lead	207.2
83	Bi	Bismuth	208.98
84	Po	Polonium	(209)
85	At	Astatine	(210)
86	Rn	Radon	(222)
87	Fr	Francium	(223)
88	Ra	Radium	(226)
89 – 103	Ac-Lr	Actinide	
104	Rf	Rutherfordium	(267)
105	Db	Dubnium	(268)
106	Sg	Seaborgium	(271)
107	Bh	Bohrium	(272)
108	Hs	Hassium	(270)
109	Mt	Meitnerium	(276)
110	Ds	Darmstadtium	(281)
111	Rg	Roentgenium	(280)
112	Cn	Copernicium	(285)
113	Nh	Nihonium	(284)
114	Fl	Flerovium	(289)
115	Mc	Moscovium	(288)
116	Lv	Livermorium	(293)
117	Ts	Tennessine	(294)
118	Og	Oganesson	(294)

Lanthanides

Z	Symbol	Name	Atomic mass
57	La	Lanthanum	138.91
58	Ce	Cerium	140.12
59	Pr	Praseodymium	140.91
60	Nd	Neodymium	144.24
61	Pm	Promethium	(145)
62	Sm	Samarium	150.36
63	Eu	Europium	151.96
64	Gd	Gadolinium	157.25
65	Tb	Terbium	158.93
66	Dy	Dysprosium	162.50
67	Ho	Holmium	164.93
68	Er	Erbium	167.26
69	Tm	Thulium	168.93
70	Yb	Ytterbium	173.05
71	Lu	Lutetium	174.97

Actinides

Z	Symbol	Name	Atomic mass
89	Ac	Actinium	(227)
90	Th	Thorium	232.04
91	Pa	Protactinium	231.04
92	U	Uranium	238.03
93	Np	Neptunium	(237)
94	Pu	Plutonium	(244)
95	Am	Americium	(243)
96	Cm	Curium	(247)
97	Bk	Berkelium	(247)
98	Cf	Californium	(251)
99	Es	Einsteinium	(252)
100	Fm	Fermium	(257)
101	Md	Mendelevium	(258)
102	No	Nobelium	(259)
103	Lr	Lawrencium	(262)

Murrieta's real hideaway

When you have escaped this chapter, check your answers to these questions by looking at the answer key on page 156.

Main character

The main "character" in this chapter is Joaquín Murrieta. Which of these "facts" about Joaquín Murrieta do you think are true? Tick.

He was Spanish.	
He was a sheriff.	
He was killed by bounty hunters.	
He lived in The American River Hotel.	
He was a Native American.	

What do you think this is?

Test your general knowledge

Choose an answer for each of the questions below.

1. Which country do you associate with the Virgin of Guadalupe?
   a. Chile
   b. Spain
   c. Mexico

2. What image appears on a pirate's flag?
   a. a devil and an angel
   b. a skull and crossbones
   c. a canon

3. What are the suits in a pack of poker cards?
   a. hearts, diamonds, clubs and spades
   b. hearts, jewels, clover leaves and coins
   c. hearts, stars, clubs and spoons

Useful words and expressions

Knowing the meaning of these words will help you escape from this chapter.

A trapdoor is a small door, usually in the floor or ceiling, that gives secret access to a place.

A deponent is somebody who gives evidence before a legal institution.

Something veritable is something true.

Frantic refers to an activity that is chaotic and fast.

Talking point

At the time of the Californian Gold Rush, law and order was often enforced by groups of armed people. Do you think there are better ways to keep order than with guns? Talk to your classmates, friends or family and share your ideas and experiences.

4-5-6: the trapdoor at the top of the staircase in the tunnel opens.

You climb up and find yourself standing in a room with no windows. The only light enters through a circular skylight.

The trapdoor in the floor suddenly closes with a bang. You pull on the rusted circular ring attached to it, but it won't open.

In the room, there's a ceramic fireplace, an iron bed frame, a dressing table with a mirror and a moth-eaten, reddish armchair.

The floor is wooden and the walls are painted a warm orange color. A two-candle chandelier without any candles hangs from the ceiling above the bed. There is a child's drawing of the Virgin of Guadalupe on the wall above the fireplace and a clock on the wall near the door.

You try the room door handle. It won't move. You check your cellphone. Still no network coverage and the battery charge is down to 30%. What is going on?

---

18 **trapdoor** a wooden door in the floor that usually leads to a cellar

You wonder if you should shout for help, but something stops you from doing so: the strange things you experienced in the tunnel between Murrieta's hideaway and this room have stimulated your curiosity and you want to find out more.

There is nothing to indicate how or even *if* you should find a way out of the room.

The room door has no keyhole, combination lock or any other device attached to it.

You look under the bed and find nothing.

You approach the dressing table and open the small drawer just under the tabletop.

Inside, there's a rolled-up piece of very thin, fragile paper, an old box of "Calavera" matches with a skull and crossbones logo, and three poker cards: the king of spades, the king of clubs and the ace of hearts.

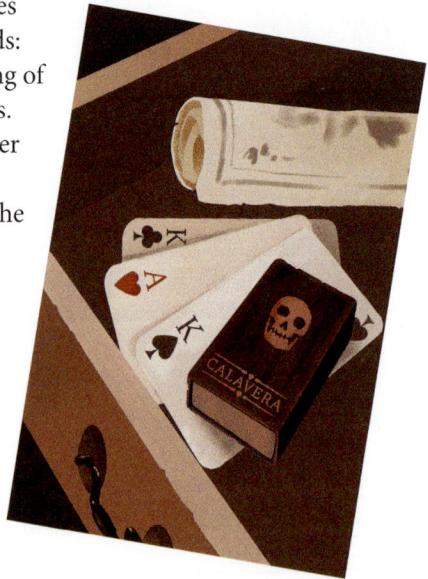

You take the roll of paper and matches out of the drawer and put them on the dressing table.

You strike one of the matches. It lights. You blow it out.

You open the roll of paper on the dressing table.

The paper is very thin.

---

26 **dressing table** a table with a mirror that you can use when you are getting yourself ready for the day

10 FUN FACTS ABOUT
JOAQUÍN MURRIETA

Fact 1: Nobody's sure where he was actually from.
Two places claim to be the place where Joaquín Murrieta was born: Quillota, in Chile, and Sonora, in Mexico.

Fact 2: Hero or villain?
To some historians, Joaquín Murrieta was a cruel, ambitious and murderous man. To others he was a hero, motivated by the unjust treatment immigrants received in California. Nobody really knows the truth …

Fact 3: Some people say he was the inspiration for fictional heroes.
Joaquín Murrieta was the subject of a play by Nobel Prize for Literature Chilean author, Pablo Neruda. However, it's not so clear if he inspired fictional heroes Zorro and Batman, as some people claim.

Fact 4: His legend was so powerful that people saw him in two or more places at the same time.
People accused Murrieta of crimes that happened hundreds of miles apart on the same day!

Fact 5: There was a price on his head.
In the spring of 1853, a $6,000 reward was offered to anybody who could kill Joaquín Murrieta and cut off his head as proof. On 25 July, that year, Los Angeles Deputy Sheriff Harry Love and his men attacked an outlaw camp in the early morning and killed eight men, including, they said, Joaquín Murrieta, whose head they cut off and preserved in a jar of brandy.

Fact 6: His head was destroyed in the 1906 San Francisco Earthquake.

Murrieta's supposed head was placed behind the bar of the Golden Nugget Saloon in San Francisco, until the building was destroyed by the 1906 San Francisco earthquake.

Fact 7: People love a villain (hero)!

Characters based on Joaquín Murrieta have appeared in 19 film, TV and radio productions, and several novels.

Fact 8: His closest allies were all called Joaquín.

Murrieta himself, along with Joaquín Ocomorenia, Joaquín Valenzuela, Joaquín Botellier, and Joaquín Carillo were said to work together in a gang called "The Five Joaquíns."

Fact 9: He still inspires people today.

Second and third generation Mexicans living in California who claim historical justice for the Mexicans that lost their fortunes because of Anglo laws during the Gold Rush, still identify with Joaquín Murrieta and his legend today.

Fact 10: He fits the folk hero stereotype perfectly.

According to many experts, a folk hero is usually of poor origin, is brave, fights oppression, is motivated by the desire to revenge a personal injustice (Joaquín Murrieta's wife was abused by Anglos when his gold mining stake was taken from him), is an astute leader, and dies (or doesn't) in mysterious circumstances. Just like Joaquín Murrieta!

THE HEAD

OF THE EVIL BANDIT

JOAQUIN

AND THE HAND OF
THREE-FINGERED JACK
TO BE EXHIBITED

AT THE
STOCKTON HOUSE
AUG. 19, 1853 - $1

ONE DAY ONLY

STATE OF CALIFORNIA – COUNTY OF SAN FRANCISCO, ss: Ignacio Lisaragga, of Sonora, being duly sworn, says: - That he has seen the alleged head of Joaquin, now on exhibition and That deponent was well acquainted with Joaquin Murrieta, and that the head as exhibited above is and was the veritable head of Joaquin Murrieta, the celebrated bandit. And further says not. IGNACIO LISARRAGA.

You take your hands off the poster and it rolls up.

You explore the room again. There is nothing else of interest.

Your phone vibrates. A message is flashing on the screen again, and the battery charge is now at 7%.

DANGER!

"Hey!" you shout, suddenly terrified. "Enough now! This is weird!"

Silence. Then you hear footsteps. Someone wearing a man's wooden-soled boots or shoes is walking from one side to the other of the room above you.

Suddenly, a red letter, "F", appears on the dressing table mirror.

"Hey, come on!" you shout.

Another red letter appears: "I".

Then: "N D A N D S A Y T H E I N V I S I B L E M E S S A G E."

As quickly as the letters have appeared, they disappear.

"Think, AD!" you tell yourself.

The letters on the mirror appear again: "F I N D A N D S A Y T H E I N V I S I B L E M E S S A G E."

The only thing you know about invisible messages is what you learned in science class three or four years ago: you can write on paper with lemon juice and use intense light to see the message.

Apart from the poker cards, the drawing of the Virgin of Guadalupe and the map and letter in your pocket, the only object in the room made out of paper is the poster celebrating the capture of Joaquín Murrieta.

You open the draw in the dressing table again and trap one end of the poster between the drawer and the table. You pull the poster open and sit on the floor underneath it.

---

9 **wooden-soled** with wood on the bottom of them

You try to use your cellphone torch, but it won't work. The

DANGER!

message is still flashing and your
battery charge is now at 4%.

You light a match and move the
flame close to the back of the poster, being careful not to burn the
old paper.

Letters appear on the paper.

You blow on the match to extinguish it before the flame burns
your fingers and you light another.

When you bring the lit match close to the back of the poster,
more letters appear. Again, you extinguish the match and light
another. Then, it occurs to you to use the burned end of the used
matches on the floor to mark the letters you see.

AGARRASIL OICANGI .ton syas
rehtruf dnA .tidnab detarbelec eht
,ateirruM niuqaoJ fo daeh elbatirev
eht saw dna si evoba detibihxe
sa daeh eht taht dna ,ateirruM
niuqaoJ htiw detniauqca llew saw
tnenoped tahT dna noitibihxe no
won ,niuqaoJ fo daeh degella eht
nees sah eh tahT - :syas ,nrows
ylud gnieb ,aronoS fo ,aggarasiL
oicangI :ss ,OCSICNARF NAS FO
YTNUOC – AINROFILAC FO
ETATS

---

8 **to extinguish** to put out

Another message appears on the dressing table mirror. WHICH MESSAGE IS IT, AD? SAY THE NUMBER. YOU HAVE ONE CHANCE.

Your cellphone has started to vibrate wildly and the footsteps you can hear in the room above you are heavier and more frantic now.

When you are satisfied that there are no more letters to find, you stand up, turn the poster over and read the message.

When you've finished doing so, three "choices" appear on the mirror.

"IT IS A LIE – 85"

"IT IS NOT TRUE – 97"

"IT IS TRUE – 124"

You say _____ and turn to page _____.

The room door opens.

Another message appears on the dressing table mirror: TAKE THE MATCHES WITH YOU.

You push the box of matches into a trouser pocket, leave the room and find yourself in a corridor. Of a hotel maybe. There was a hotel on the map your dad gave you, wasn't there?

The door you've just opened closes behind you.

You see that on the outside the door has no handle and looks like just a part of the corridor wall. It's so amazing, you think, how cleverly the secret door into the room has been hidden behind a painting of miners in the mountains with a gold panning contraption you remember from your school project and is called a *long tom*.

You see a door in the corridor, with the number you found on the poster and walk towards it.

It all goes back to the river

When you've escaped this chapter, check your answers to these questions by looking at the answer key on page 156.

The American River Hotel
In this chapter you leave The American River Hotel, but what can you remember about this mysterious place?

How many rooms did AD enter?	
Who owned the hotel?	
What was the first room AD entered?	
What was the last room AD entered?	
What did AD hear happening upstairs?	

What do you think this is?

Test your general knowledge
Choose an answer for each of the questions below.

1. Which city in Germany did Albrecht Dürer grow up in?
   a. Bochum
   b. Munich
   c. Nuremberg

2. What do you call a place in a river where it divides into two?
   a. a split
   b. a fork
   c. a separation

3. What color is cobalt?
   a. yellow
   b. red
   c. blue

Useful words and expressions

Knowing the meaning of these words will help you escape from this chapter.

A current is the constant movement of river water below the surface capable of pulling a person along.

To move downstream in a river is to move towards the sea.

When the penny drops we understand a situation that we previously didn't understand.

To carbon date an object means to establish how old something is by analyzing the radiocarbon in the object.

Talking point

The value of works of art like those created by Albrecht Dürer can be tens of millions of euros. Meanwhile, millions of people on all continents live in poverty. Do you think this is fair? Talk to your classmates, friends or family and share your ideas and experiences.

On the other side of the door is the crumbling lobby of The American River Hotel.

You open the roll of paper from the shotgun barrel on the reception counter.

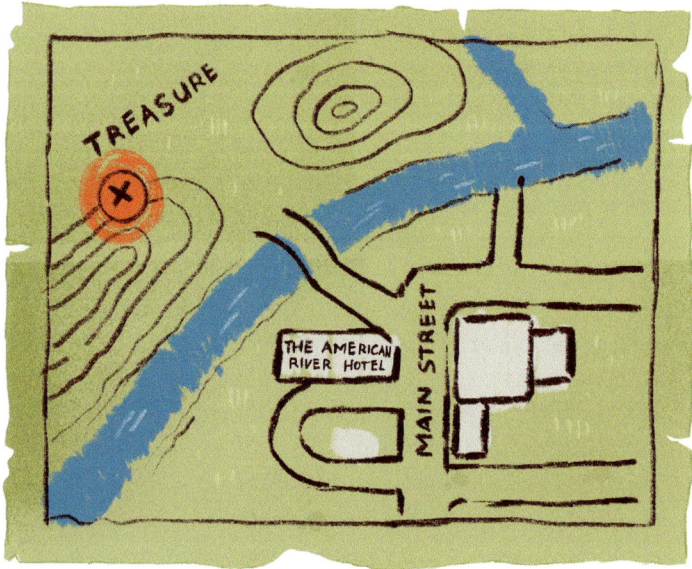

Network coverage returns, your battery charge is at 100% and your cellphone begins to beep as it receives messages from both your parents, from George and even from Selena.

You take a few seconds to write to them all.

I'm okay. 🥺

You look at the map. There is an "X" on the other side of a mountain.

To get there you must cross the American River North Fork, via a bridge.

With your cellphone still beeping with new messages, you roll up the map, leave The American River Hotel behind you and run as fast as your legs can take you in the direction of the river.

It feels good to sense the spring air on your face, to see the mountains and the cobalt-blue sky and to smell the gray dust beneath your feet rising to your nostrils.

You leave Miner's Haven behind you and reach the river, but where there should be a bridge, there is none. Your heart sinks.

Then you think of the treasure, gold surely. Maybe gold the assayer, Jean-Pierre Aurelian, hid nearly two hundred years ago. Gold that could change you and your family's life forever!

The river is perhaps twenty meters wide and the current doesn't look too strong. In your head, you hear the voice of Robert White, the dying gold miner from The American Hotel: "And their hope never dies, Blanche, because the river water washes it clean every day. Every single day."

You walk into the river, with your cellphone in one hand and the treasure map from the assayer's room in the other.

And when the icy river water is up to your chest, you realize that the river is deeper than you imagined and that there is indeed a strong current, pushing and pulling on your knees and hips, trying to drag you under and downstream, as if you were a log that had fallen into the river from one of the oak trees. You try to swim, but the current takes you downstream and you panic and the current pulls you down into the water and then it's your mom's voice that you hear: "In life, sometimes it's better just to let yourself be dragged downstream, AD, than to fight and be drowned."

So, you relax and let the river take control. You just concentrate on keeping your head above water, until, eventually, the river itself throws you onto a sandy shore on the outside of a bend.

---

8 **your heart sinks** you are very disappointed – 22 **downstream** further down the river

Your phone's waterproof and is OK. It beeps. Your dad has sent you his location. Which is just as well, as the treasure map is gone.

You open the location on your maps App and begin walking.

You walk for about ten minutes through an oak wood before you smell the wood smoke.

Then, after ten minutes more walking, you *see* the wood smoke.

In fact you come out of the trees you see them, all of them. All your family members who live in the United States, George and the rest of your closest friends, a few teammates from basketball, your nicest neighbors, your drawing teacher, all gathered around three picnic tables and a barbecue.

And as you approach them, tired now, and cold from the river water, but so happy to see everyone, they all start singing "Happy Birthday".

So, this was the treasure `A`wa`y and Jean-Pierre Aurelian were talking about!

It makes perfect sense (though some gold would have been nice too!).

Selena, Jake and Elmore come running towards you and envelop you in a hug.

Then Selena says you smell bad because of the river water and gives you one of *those* looks.

You just laugh and hug the three of them more tightly as you see your mom and dad walking towards you, smiling, and they join in the hug too, and everybody else claps and then the music starts and you walk towards your birthday party hand-in-hand with your family.

And then, for the second time in a short while, the penny drops and you say to your mom and dad: "You two set that up, didn't you?"

"Nope. Just me," says your mom.

---

28 **the penny drops** when you realize what has been going on – 29 **to set sth up** to organize sth

"Rosa wanted you to have something special for your birthday party," says your dad.

"Was it *very* wowza?" asks Jake.

"*Très*, Jake! *Très* wowza!" you answer.

And Selena pretends to look pleased for you, even though you expect she's probably jealous.

The people at the party are still applauding. As you walk past them you see the actresses that played both a young and old `A`wa`y are among them as well as the man that just played Jean-Pierre Aurelian.

Your brothers and sisters guide you towards a tent and wait outside while you change into dry clothes and you're happy to have their company.

"Mom and Dad wanted you to know who our ancestors are," says Jake, from somewhere outside the tent.

"Yeah, in one way or another, we're descended from lots of the people who lived or stayed at that hotel where you had your adventure. Mom has the family tree!" explains Elmore.

"We mi-ss-ed you, AD!" shouts Jake.

"Yeah," adds Selena. "But really they wanted to try out the new expensive immersive experience gadgets they've been buying, too, for their business."

You pay no attention to your sister's observation, leave the tent and the four of you walk back to the party, where you shake everyone's hand.

"Joaquín Murrieta," say both the actors who gave California's most feared Gold Rush bandit his young man's voice and the one who gave him his older voice.

You blush as everybody turns to look at you and then a murmur you can't quite interpret runs through the party.

---

7 **to applaud** to clap – 21 **immersive experience** a planned experience that pulls you into a new or augmented reality – 27 **bandit** robber – 30 **murmur** a soft noise

"Can I be the one to tell AD about his *other* present, Mom, Dad?" asks Selena.

"Of course you can, Selena," says your dad.

"Come and sit at the table, AD," says your dad.

Ceremoniously, your dad picks up a metal box, the size of a pizza box, from the table and hands it to Selena, who hands it to you.

You open the box.

Inside there is an engraving in the style of Albrecht Dürer, depicting a man panning for gold in a river.

5 **ceremoniously** in a very formal way – 9 **engraving** artwork in which an image is cut into a smooth surface

10 FUN FACTS ABOUT
ALBRECHT DÜRER

Fact 1: He was from a Hungarian family.
Dürer's original, Hungarian surname meant "doormaker". His father changed this surname to "Türer" when he moved his family to Nuremberg, then, influenced by the dialect spoken in Nuremberg, he changed it to "Dürer".

Fact 2: He had lots of help!
Once he had become famous, Dürer only drew the designs for his engravings, using the knowledge he had learned about the process. His helpers did the rest!

Fact 3: A strange fact about the most famous engraving in History
In 1515, Dürer made a woodcut of a rhinoceros. When he did so, he had only read a description and seen a sketch by another artist. Dürer never actually saw a rhinoceros!

Fact 4: He was a stargazer.
In 1515 Dürer and Konrad Heinfogel produced the first printed celestial maps.

Fact 5: He was great at networking!
Dürer was a good friend of both Raphael and Leonardo da Vinci!

Fact 6: He had lots of brothers and sisters.
Dürer had seventeen brothers and sisters.

Fact 7: He worked for very important people.
In 1512, the Holy Roman Emperor, Maximilian became Dürer's patron.

Fact 8: He was a young starter.
Dürer made his first self-portrait at the age of thirteen.

Fact 9: He was good at branding.
He invented a logo, containing an "A" and a "D", which he
incorporated in his works of Art. This was his brand.

Fact 10: You can visit his home.
In the house he bought in 1509, in Nuremberg, there is a
museum dedicated to Dürer.

Thinking the image is a reproduction, you say, "I've never seen
this one, thanks."

Your dad smiles.

"Nobody's seen it since 1854, AD," he says. "We've sent it to the
relevant experts had it x-rayed and had it carbon dated."

An expectant silence falls on everyone at the party.

"You mean … it's an original?" you ask.

"Sure is. It's a lost Dürer, AD. Your mom found it in Uwe
Dresler's suitcase in his room at The American Hotel. I guess old
Uwe brought it with him when he emigrated from Nuremberg.
They used to pan for gold there, too, you see, way back in the
day."

"Dad's had it insured, of course," says Selena.

You close your eyes.

When you open them again, everyone is still there, staring
at you and at the open box Selena is holding; and everything,
everything, your past, your family's past, your neighbors, your
friends, the love in your heart, is so, *so* real. And there and
then, you decide to draw and to write about everything that has

---

16 **to have sth carbon dated** to find out how old an artwork is – 21 **to emigrate** to leave
the country you are from in order to live somewhere else – 22 **to pan for gold** to look for
gold – 29 **there and then** at that moment

happened to you today, and maybe turn it into a book, an Escape Adventure, perhaps, so that people from wherever, people you'll never even meet, probably, can share your experience *right by and even* in The American River Hotel.

This book, for example …

"Food's ready!" shouts Jake and Elmore, at exactly the same time.

Seeing the elephant

When you've escaped this chapter, check your answers to these questions by looking at the answers key on page 156.

Main characters

The main characters in this chapter are A`wa`y and Uwe Dresler. Guess if the facts correspond to Uwe or A`Wa`y.

From Nuremberg	
Helps AD	
Once lived in Brooklyn, NYC	
A Native American	
A photographer	

What do you think this is?

Test your general knowledge

Choose an answer for each of the questions below.
1. For gold miners, "to see the elephant" meant:
   a. to die
   b. to see something frightening
   c. to imagine their dreams had come true

2. In 1849 there were 100 houses in Sacramento, California.
   In 1851, there were:
   a. 1,000
   b. 10,000
   c. 50

3. What does a lithographer make?
   a. alcohol
   b. clothes
   c. prints

Useful words and expressions
Knowing the meaning of these words will help you escape from this chapter.

To reckon is to calculate, estimate or guess using some evidence.

To do or say something brusquely is to do or say something quickly and aggressively.

To be homesick is to have an enormous desire to return home.

To travel overland is the opposite to travelling oversea.

Talking point

In this chapter, A`wa`y reminds AD that Selena said that ghosts are for losers. Do you believe in ghosts? Have you or anyone you know seen a ghost? Talk to your classmates, friends or family and share your ideas and experiences.

The door of room 85 closes behind you.

As you approach door 56, the window at the end of the corridor darkens and a woman appears under the window.

More intrigued than afraid now, you don't move.

You expect the walls of the corridor to show you something about where and how the woman lived, but nothing happens. She just stands there, smiling at you.

"Welcome to Miner's Haven, AD," the woman says. "We've already met. You saw the village where I was born in the tunnel, remember?"

The woman pauses and you're not sure if you should reply.

"Yes," you say and suddenly feel the desire to run, far away.

"Don't be afraid, AD, I'm not a ghost."

The woman opens her eyes a little wider and smiles, knowingly.

"And anyway, ghosts are for losers, right?"

---

19 **to approach** to come close to – 21 **intrigued** very interested

It feels strange to know that the ethereal figure before you knows exactly what Selena said when you arrived in Miner's Haven.

"My name's A`wa`y, which means "Moon," like Selena, but you can call me Mona. They're all okay, by the way, your family. Of course, Selena insisted they check out McQueen's Store. Not much there to see now though, but she's got a fine imagination that girl, she's a moonchild, after all, and she enjoyed it. They've gone back to the car to get something to eat. They reckon you've gone exploring. You'll be with them again soon enough."

You are surprised at the sense of relief you feel to know that your family is well.

A`wa`y smiles at you again, understandingly.

"So, AD," she says, with a voice that reminds you of a teacher switching from relaxed to stern mode, "you're probably wondering what you're doing here."

"Yes," you mumble.

"I'll tell you when you finish with the next room. Fifty-six wasn't it? You'll be fine in there, AD. In my mind's eye, I can see the man who last used that room as if it were yesterday. A handsome sort. A German, from Nuremberg. Such a wonderful talent for drawing, AD. Just like you."

Light comes back into the corridor through the window above where A`wa`y, or Mona, is standing. She disappears and the door at the end of the corridor on the right clicks open.

Now you know that you've got a (strange, but hey, there's nothing normal about any of this) "guide," you feel less anxious and walk towards door 56.

---

1 **ethereal** ghostly – 9 **to reckon** to think – 17 **to mumble** to speak unclearly

The window in this room is on the same wall as the high window that illuminates the corridor and is covered by two pink curtains.

There's a bed without a mattress, as in the previous two rooms, and the same dressing table.

There's also the same drawer and the same armchair.

To the left of the door, which has closed, of course, there's a wardrobe.

You check your phone and see that nothing has changed, except the battery charge is now at 17%.

You open the wardrobe doors.

On a shelf in the wardrobe is a sort of suitcase made from wool and leather, with the name Dresler printed on it: your own surname … By now, nothing surprises you.

You pick the suitcase up and discover it's heavy and, for a moment, you imagine it's full of gold.

You feel an enormous rush of excitement!

You put the suitcase down on the metal bed frame and when you do so it makes a sound that lets you know its bottom is also made of metal, which is why it's so heavy.

You feel disappointed and a little stupid.

You open the suitcase.

Inside is an envelope, with no writing on it, and a book, called *Ratgeber für Auswanderer nach Kalifornien.*

You pick the book up and look through it, but can see no clues and you don't understand German anyway, because at home you speak English and Spanish. You take your cellphone and the box of matches out of your back pockets and put them on the floor next to where you eventually sit, with your back against the wall next to the dressing table. You feel a little tired now.

You take the envelope out of the bag, open it and discover an unfinished letter.

You read the letter.

Room 56, The American River Hotel   May 1, 1851

Miner's Haven
Sacramento

Dear Love,

I have been here in Miner's Haven for a week now.

I try to stay enthusiastic, but it's difficult. I feel homesick
all the time. Not for Germany, or Nuremberg, no; for Brooklyn,
because wherever you and little Hans are, Mina, that's my
home. By the way, I hope you like my sketch of the Edelweiss
flower. To romantic Germans, it's a symbol of eternal love.

I came to Miner's Haven with my friend Marco, to make
sketches of gold-diggers at work to show to Herr Nahl and Herr
Wenderwoth when we get back to Sacramento. They told me that
if they like the sketches they might give me work in their studio!
And guess what? There's a painting by Nahl and Wenderworth
in the hotel corridor here. I will try to draw a copy of it and send
it to you in another letter.

I pray to God that Herr Nahl and Herr Wenderwoth like my
sketches, Mina.

If I'm in luck, I can start earning a real living and we
can be together again. I'd love to make lithographs from the
sketches, but, as you know, I don't have my equipment here and
everything in California is so, so expensive!

Miner's Haven is a typical mining village. There's not much to do but search for gold and visit the saloon. Lots of newcomers arrive every day, hoping to "see the elephant," which means wanting to experience the excitement all 49ers feel, I suppose, when they see gold for themselves. I guess that's why a lot of the men (there are only six women in the village, Mina, apart from the ones who "work" in the saloon, which I haven't visited, but Marco has) walk around looking at the ground, to see if they can see any "color" as the miners who pan for gold call it.

Before I left Sacramento, Marco and I had a very nice afternoon listening to a sort of Bavarian band playing in the center of town. In general, German-speakers in California are well-liked, because we can be serious when needed, but also know how to have fun. And there are so many men in Sacramento from Austria, Bavaria, Baden, Prussia, and Germany itself, Mina, as well as others born in Switzerland.

There's even a town, called Tuleberg, in the South, which was founded by a German who used to work on Sutter's Fort, where the gold fever started. I haven't been to either place yet. I'll wait until you come, meine Liebe!

Sacramento really is amazing, Mina. An old man I met from Bavaria told me that in June two years ago there were 100 houses in the town, all wooden of course, but in August, there were 1000! And the town hasn't stopped growing since then, either.

But I feel safer out here, Mina. There are floods, dysentery and cholera in Sacramento and the Anglos (sorry to use that word, Mina, I know you're an Anglo, too) sometimes arrest us Germans for no reason at all. In time, I'm sure it'll be better organized and more civil, especially as California's a State now. We'll be fine, Mina!

I've decided that you must come by land, not sea. The passage by ship doesn't worry me. I know you are a brave woman. But crossing the south of Mexico or Panama is just too dangerous, Mina.

One day I'll tell you everything that happened to me down there. When the time comes, I'd like you and your brother John to come on the overland trails. Trust me, Mina. It's for the best.

I think of you every day, my love, and of little Hans. And every day I try to improve myself as much as I can. The same old man from Bavaria who told me about the houses in Sacramento explained to me I should remember this: a bar of iron costs $1, for example. If the iron bar is made into horseshoes it's worth $2. Make the iron bar into needles and it's worth $1000. And if you make springs for watches with the iron bar, it's worth $150,000.

Why did he tell me that, Mina? Because, the old man said, a person is worth what they make of their own talents. And right here's the best place in the world to do that, Mina. Unless you're a Native Indian, that is, because

10 FUN FACTS ABOUT
HOW THE CALIFORNIAN GOLD RUSH CHANGED THE UNITED STATES

Fact 1: Communication networks developed.
One of the first American mail services, the Pony Express, was created to send mail and parcels from California to the Midwest of the United States.

Fact 2: Farming in California suffered. The mercury used in gold-mining processes flowed down rivers, damaging river water used for agriculture.

Fact 3: California soon became a state.
Before the Gold Rush, California was isolated from the rest of the United States. Then, in part because of the arrival of hundreds of thousands of people from the East of the United States, it soon became a state.

Fact 4: Prices went up across the United States.
So much gold changed the economy across the United States!

Fact 5: It changed the landscape of California.
The use of hydraulic mining technology was so harmful to the environment that it was prohibited by law in 1884.

Fact 6: Lots of trees were cut down.
A tree planting and cutting industry was born, because many of the processes used to extract gold needed wood.

Fact 7: Gold money helped the home economies of gold diggers.
Money sent or taken home by Anglos helped build the economies in the places in the United States that the 49ers had left to participate in the Gold Rush.

Fact 8: The role of women back home changed.
The seeds of feminism were sown because the women left at home by gold diggers who moved to California had to manage farms and businesses alone.

Fact 9: If you're going to San Francisco …
San Francisco slowly began to compete with New York as the most important city in the United States.

Fact 10: The American Dream became real.
The idea of a free land of opportunity was represented forever by the Californian Gold Rush!

The footsteps in the room above you start again, but this time you can hear two people moving around and furniture being moved, brusquely.

Your phone vibrates frantically. You look at it.

DANGER! it says (the battery is at 1%. You have no idea what would happen if the battery died).

You hear a gunshot in the room above and the sound of a body falling to the floor.

You look at the letter again.

Maybe there's a message written in it, as there was on the back of the Murrieta's head poster. You read the letter again and notice that the mistaken letters are mixed up and form three words.

Listen to the clue!

Are these words, _____ _____ _____, the number of the next room? You certainly hope so …

A time tunnel

When you've escaped this chapter, check your answers to these questions by looking at the answer key on page 156.

What do you know about AD so far?
Are these statements about AD true or false?

AD finds Art boring.	
AD has been to Miner's Haven before.	
AD has German and Italian ancestors.	
AD knows nothing about the California Gold Rush.	
AD's home is in Los Gatos.	

Who do you think this is?

Can you hear the numbers?
To escape from this chapter, you need to pay attention to the syllables in words that sound like numbers. An example is *ten* and ea*ten*.

Can you hear the two-, three- or four-digit numbers in these sentences?
a. Are you going to come with us, too?
b. Let's hurry, before it's too late!
c. Sorry, I've forgotten your name!
d. I ate all the cake before you got here!
e. Food, tent, sleeping bag: the basics for a camping trip.

Useful words and expressions

Knowing the meaning of these words will help you escape from this chapter.

If something is indecipherable it is impossible to understand. The Anglos were the people who participated in the Gold Rush who were of European descendancy.
A ladder is similar to stairs but can usually be moved around. When something happens in a flash, it happens very quickly and unexpectedly.

Talking point

In this chapter, we learn that in California, in 1850, it was very difficult for Mexican, Peruvian, Chilean or Chinese people to make money legally. Why do you think this was? Talk to your classmates, friends or family and share your ideas and experiences.

You enter 68 into the combination lock, remove the lock and open the wardrobe doors.

Inside, there's a wooden trapdoor, with words written on it: "tskumu," "yətipake'es" and "yəti'iš koṁ."

You climb into the wardrobe and the doors close behind you.

You try to open them but can't.

Your phone stops vibrating. You take it out of your pocket and see the battery charge is now up to 80%. There is, however, no network coverage.

You turn on your cellphone torch and see that there's another three-digit combination lock on the trapdoor. You check the photo of the reassembled circle number you sent to George and decode the digits you need, "tskumu," "yətipake'es," and "yəti'iš koṁ," 4-5-6, and the combination lock opens.

You open the trap door and climb down the ladder underneath it with the help of your cellphone torch.

On the wall to the right of the foot of the ladder, there's a light switch. You flick it on and white light floods your eyes. Your pupils narrow and you see that you are at one end of a tunnel wide and high enough for you to walk along it. The tunnel is about a hundred meters long and the walls, roof and floor are the same gray as the land above your head.

You're afraid but intrigued.

Suddenly, a voice emerges from your cellphone. A quiet, whispering, girl's voice with an accent you can't identify.

The voice says, "We've been waiting for you, AD. Don't be scared."

In a flash, the light in the tunnel changes to a mixture of green and violet.

"Walk forward," says the girl's voice, still coming from your cellphone.

You look back up at the ladder towards the trapdoor that would take you back into the wardrobe in Murrieta's Hideaway.

---

12 **to reassemble** to put sth back together – 19 **pupil** the black part in the middle of your eye

It's closed and something tells you there would be no way to open it, even if you wanted to.

"Walk forward, AD," repeats the girl's gentle voice, and you obey.

As you do so, the light in the tunnel changes to blinding gold and the walls and roof of the tunnel are suddenly covered with images of people, Native American people, men, women and children, young and old, stood before their strange houses made from branches, staring at you with a question, the same indecipherable question, in their eyes.

Then everything goes quiet and dark.

You turn your cellphone torch on again.

You take three steps towards the end of the tunnel and a Native American girl, of about your age, appears on the wall you're walking towards.

"Don't be afraid, AD," says the girl.

---

3 **to obey** to do what you are told to do

10 FUN FACTS ABOUT
THE CHUMASH

Fact 1: The Chumash tribe is very, very old!
The Chumash are one of the oldest tribes in North America.
Skeletons of Chumash ancestors have been found that are
more than 13,000 years old.

Fact 2: Men or women could be Chumash chiefs.
A Chumash chief was called a *wot*. The *wot* was a hereditary
position, which means it was passed on through the family.
The *wot* could be a man or a woman.

Fact 3: They were one of the first people to meet Europeans.
The Portuguese explorer Juan Rodríguez met the Chumash in
1542.

Fact 4: They had a special relationship with animals.
The Chumash believed that when death appeared on Earth,
some animals rose into the sky to escape death and became the
Sun, the Moon, the Morning Star and the Evening Star.

Fact 5: They didn't like fighting.
The Chumash did not wage war often, but if a conflict with
another tribe happened, the rivals lined up facing one another.
Then, one member from each side shot an arrow at the other
side. When just one person was killed, the battle was over.

Fact 6: They loved shells!
The name Chumash means "person who uses shells as money."

Fact 7: They loved playing games!
There favorite game was *tikawich*, which was similar to
hockey!

The girl's voice echoes through the tunnel. She points to her right and disappears. Then the tunnel fills with white light again.

You walk forwards until you reach the place where you saw the girl and see that the tunnel continues to your left and that where it ends there is a short staircase, cut from the gray earth.

First, you take a photograph of the staircase. Then you climb it.

At the top there's a trapdoor, just like the one in the wardrobe in Murrieta's Hideaway.

In the middle of the trapdoor, there's a square with numbers on it, which you take a photo of.

You press the numbers on the trapdoor at random and nothing happens.

"AD."

You hear the voice of the Native American girl behind you again and turn to look.

There's nobody there.

"Read the letter, AD," says the girl's voice.

You try pressing more numbers on the trapdoor. Nothing happens.

"AD, read the letter."

The voice is now that of a young man with a heavy Mexican accent.

You turn around. There's nobody there.

"The letter will tell you the numbers you need," continues the young man's voice, which you realize is coming from your cellphone.

You remove the letter you found in Murrieta's Hideaway from the back pocket of your pants.

You sit on one of the steps of the stone staircase, put your cellphone down beside you, open the envelope and begin to read.

The voice coming from your cellphone reads with you.

They haven't forgotten about you, hermano.

Don't be frightened, but there's a price on your head, so you must lie low.

Making money legally is almost impossible if you're Mexican, Peruvian or Chilean: "greasers" they call us now, or "tarheads", if you're Chinese.

The Anglos want all the gold, but we won't be beaten.

Be careful, I'll look after the family the best I can.

Stay strong!
J.T.

"You heard four numbers, AD," says the young man's voice.
"You need to add these numbers up to escape from the tunnel."
Silence.
You read the letter again and, in your head, you "hear" the four
numbers and you add them up.
You stand up, put the letter back in the pocket of your pants,
press two digits on the trapdoor and …

Listen to the clue!

Listen. Can you "hear" four numbers?
_____. Add these numbers up.
The result is the page number you need.

Sleepyhead

When you've escaped this chapter, check your answers to these questions by looking at the answer key on page 156.

What do you know about wildflowers?

Wildflowers are important in this chapter. Which of these do you think are real wildflower names?

Oracle oak	
California coffeeberry	
Devil's ice	
Wild cucumber	
Lazy Mary	

What do you think this is?

Test your general knowledge

Choose an answer for each of the questions below.

1. What was a Chumash house called?
    a. An `op
    b. An `up
    c. An `ap

2. Why did native American Indians dress in animal skins to hunt?
   a. To keep them warm
   b. To smell like the animals they were hunting
   c. To ask for help from the gods

3. What is the technical term for stories that explain how the world was formed?
   a. mundimyths
   b. globomyths
   c. creation myths

Useful words and expressions

Knowing the meaning of these words will help you escape from this chapter.

A nickname is a name people use to refer to people that is not their real name.

To cry disconsolately is to cry without anybody being able to comfort you.

A misprinted page contains several errors.

To etch is to mark a surface with letters, shapes or lines.

Talking point

As a result of inflation, the price of basic things goes up. During the California Gold Rush, the rate of inflation was very high. What is the rate of inflation in your country? What effect does this have on people's lives? Talk to your classmates, friends or family and share your ideas and experiences.

In the corridor again, the first thing you notice is that the room numbers you managed to memorize have actually changed.

The door into room 97 closes and you feel afraid and disorientated.

You look at your phone. It's now 15:00. Will you ever escape from The American Hotel? You start making your way towards the door with 77 on it.

"Hello again, AD."

You look behind you towards where 'A`wa`y's voice seems to be coming from.

There's nobody there.

"Shu`nu and Leqte, my mother tried to build an `ap when we arrived in Miner's Haven, AD, but they couldn't find bullrush reeds and we lived in a tent, then a shack, like everyone else.

"That meant that instead of a cozy Chumash shelter made by arranging willow poles pushed into the ground in a circle and bending the poles at the top to form a dome that we tied willow branches to, then covered with overlapping layers of bullrush, we lived in a drafty windowless, wooden box that let the rain and snow in.

"We missed our `ap, AD, especially Shu`nu, who also missed the sauna at the old village, where the men would sit around a fire in the ground dressed as deer letting the herbal smoke impregnate their skin and hair so they could graze alongside the deer until they were in range to use their arrows and could hunt one.

"That's where Shu`nu got his nickname, AD. In that sauna, because he'd always fall asleep."

'Shu`nu,' you remember, means 'Sleepyhead.'

"And we missed our food, too, AD. When we lived on the coast, before the Gold Rush, we ate clams and mussels and abalone and venison and we'd make shellfish soup with acorn flour. But here, in Miner's Haven we were forced to eat pork and beans, dried

---

4 **disorientated** lost – 13 **bullrush reeds** plants that usually grow by a river – 19 **drafty** letting in air – 30 **clam** a kind of shellfish – 30 **mussel** a kind of shellfish – 30 **abalone** a kind of shellfish – 31 **venison** the meat from deer – 31 **acorn** the fruit of an oak tree

apples and griddle cakes made from cornmeal, flour, baking soda, salt, sugar, buttermilk, oil, and egg just to survive and everything was so, so expensive and sometimes I didn't eat, so that my little brothers and sisters could. And my mother and father grew sadder and sadder and stopped believing in our stories, our Chumash stories, AD, so *I* had to tell them to my brothers and sisters.

"Like the story about how there are two brothers in the upper world who sometimes play our hoop-and-pole game, where one player rolls the hoop and the other runs after it and tries to throw a pole through it, and it is the noise of the hoop rolling that causes thunder …

DID YOU KNOW?

10 FUN FACTS ABOUT THE NATIVE AMERICANS

Fact 1: America existed before Colombus!
When Christopher Colombus "discovered" the American continent, it is estimated that 50 million Native Americans were already living there!

Fact 2: Linguistic variety
175 indigenous languages are spoken in the United States.

Fact 3: Top Secret!
During World War II, Native Americans were employed to communicate top secret information using the Navajo language.

Fact 4: The biggest tribe
The Apache Nation is the largest Native American tribe at the present time and has a population of approximately 57,000 people.

Fact 5: All walks of life
Maria Tallchief, whose father was a member of the Osage Nation, was the first American to dance with the Paris Opera Ballet and the Bolshoi Theater in Moscow and was regarded as one of the greatest dancers in the world in the 1960s and 70s.

Fact 6: Sporting legends
Jim Thorpe, perhaps the greatest athlete of all time, was a member of the Sac and Fox Nations.

Fact 7: Cultural variety
The United States government recognizes 600 Native American Tribes.

Fact 8: Linguistic heritage
More than half of US states have names based on Native languages, such as Connecticut, Utah, and Kentucky.

Fact 9: An Indian eagle
When the United States was formally constituted, Benjamin Franklin chose the Iroquois bald eagle as the country's national symbol.

Fact 10: Two amazing musicians had Native American ancestry
Elvis Presley had a Cherokee great-great-great grandmother and Jimi Hendrix a Cherokee grandmother!

"But then I started forgetting our stories too."

Silence.

You wait, buy A`wa`y says nothing more and you open the door to room 77.

The shape of the room is the same as Murrieta's, but the only furniture is a small wooden table and a chair, over which hangs a chandelier with four lit candles.

On the table there is a book, "Selected Californian Wild Flowers", by Saul Gregson, and a leather-cased travelling alarm clock, stopped, of course, at five o'clock.

There is also a pencil.

A bookmark would seem to indicate that you should start examining the book at the page indicated.

You open the book where the bookmark indicates and examine the following, misprinted, text:

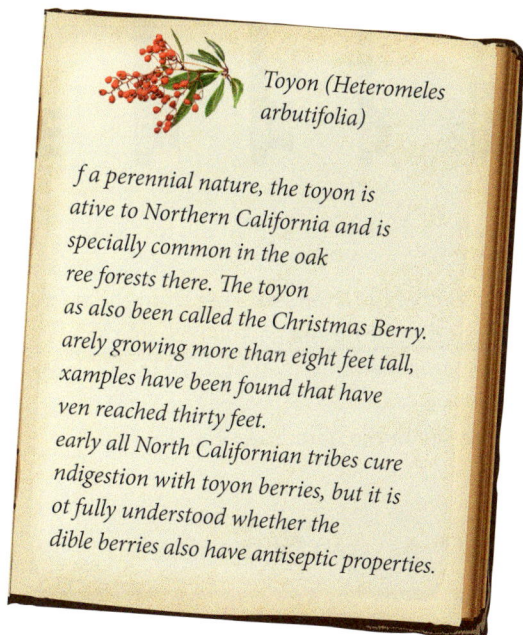

Toyon (Heteromeles arbutifolia)

f a perennial nature, the toyon is
ative to Northern California and is
specially common in the oak
ree forests there. The toyon
as also been called the Christmas Berry.
arely growing more than eight feet tall,
xamples have been found that have
ven reached thirty feet.
early all North Californian tribes cure
ndigestion with toyon berries, but it is
ot fully understood whether the
dible berries also have antiseptic properties.

You stand up and walk around the room then sit back down.

You check the text in the book again. The clue must be on the marked pages somewhere.

Your cellphone begins to vibrate. You take it out of your pocket, see the message **DANGER!** , see that you have 2% battery charge, hear a baby crying disconsolately in the room above you and a woman's voice saying, "Do something Mona, please. She's dying! Do something!" As you listen, you notice an envelope that has been pushed under the door. There is silence and your phone stops vibrating.

"You have one opportunity to try one key!" is written on the envelope. You pick it up, open it and find five keys inside, all of which are identical, except for the numbers etched onto them.

You go back to the book and read the text again.

You look at the letters missing from the start of each line and find three numbers. You pick up the key with this number etched into it and return to the door.

You try the key in the door lock. The door opens.

Listen to the clue!

Fishhooks

When you've escaped this chapter, check your answers to these
questions by looking at the answer key on page 156.

What do you know about Joaquín Murrieta so far?

Which of these facts about Joaquín Murrieta are true?

He was a doctor.	
He came to California from Mexico with some of his family.	
He was the most wanted man in California.	
He died when his horse fell into a river.	
He was a hero for some people.	

What do you think this is?

Test your Math

To escape this chapter, you'll need to use some simple Math.
Work out the correct answer for these equations.

1. 133 divided by 3.5.
    a. 36
    b. 30
    c. 38

2. 380 multiplied by 5, divided by 2, plus 765.
   a. 1715
   b. 1815
   c. 1851

3. The sum of the digits in 1849, multiplied by 2, plus 2.
   a. 44
   b. 36
   c. 46

Useful words and expressions
Knowing the meaning of these words will help you escape from this chapter.

To behead someone is to cut their head from their body.

To start from scratch is to begin something from zero.

To disguise yourself means to wear clothes and makeup that hide your appearance.

A scrapbook is a sort of album where you keep texts and images connected to a topic that interests you.

Talking point

At the end of his life, Joaquín Murrieta made a living by playing a gambling game called Three Card Monte. What do you think about gambling? Is it healthy? Talk to your classmates, friends or family and share your ideas and experiences.

Light enters from a window at the end of the corridor. The window is too high for you to see through.

You look for a door with 85 written on it.

The window at the end of the corridor darkens, as does the corridor, until you can't see a thing.

You hear a voice.

"Mexico."

It feels like the person speaking is behind you. You turn around. There's nobody there: just a wall without a window at the other end of the corridor.

"It moves me to see you, AD," says the voice and you realize that the person speaking to you is the same young man who read the letter to you in the tunnel, only older now.

"Nearly one hundred and fifty years have passed since I died, AD. Not beheaded, no, no. They never caught Joaquín Murrieta."

The corridor floods with red, then white then green light: the colors of the Mexican flag. An eagle with a snake in its mouth flies down the wall to your right.

Then, from the floor and up the walls between the doors, mustard plants start growing, quickly, filling the corridor with yellow flowers.

"That's 'El Camino Real,' AD. The trail the Missionary Fathers laid between the mission forts they established so they could evangelize the Indians of California, the real losers in the whole Gold Rush, the folk that suffered slavery, famine, discrimination and theft while the Anglos, the gold-diggers, the pioneers, the settlers, the newcomers tried, and mostly failed, to make their fortune on land that used to belong to the Native Indians.

"When they were making the trail, AD, the Missionary Fathers threw mustard seeds on the ground on both sides of it so that when the plants grew, the trail shone like gold."

The corridor is beautiful.

---

24 **to evangelize** to make sb else believe in Christianity

Fact 1: There are *lots* of Mexican-born Americans in the US.

In 1910 about 20,000 Mexican immigrants entered the United States. By 1920, 100,000 Mexican immigrants entered every year. In 2022, there were approximately 12,000,000 people born in Mexico living in the United States.

Fact 2: ¡Hola!

The United States is the fourth largest Spanish-speaking country in the world.

Fact 3: Ride it, cowboy!

What we think of as American cowboy culture first arrived in the United States thanks to Mexican cowboys.

Fact 4: There are many famous Mexican Americans!

Selena Gomez and Camila Cabello are both Mexican Americans!

Fact 5: Food, glorious food!

Chili con carne, fajitas, salsa, tortilla chips, corn chips, chimichangas, quesadillas, burritos and nachos are all variations on traditional (and quite different in their original version) Mexican dishes.

Fact 6: Spanglish spoken.

Spanglish is a mixture of Spanish and English, often spoken by Mexican immigrants who, sometimes just for fun, make English words sound Spanish. Examples include: emailear *(to email)*, twittear *(to tweet)*, wachar *(to watch)*, and parquear *(to park)*.

Fact 7: A land of DREAMers.
Illegal immigrants from Mexico (and other countries)
who arrive in the United States as children are
often referred to as DREAMers, because of the
Development, Relief, and Education for Alien Minors
Act: a group of laws designed to help these young
immigrants dreaming of a better life, but never passed
by Congress.

**Fact 8: Everyday life in the United States depends on
Mexican workers.**
According to the U.S. Department of Labor, by 2030,
35.9 million workers in the United States will be of
Mexican origin and will represent 43% of the workers
in farming, fishing and forestry jobs; 37.9% of the
workers in cleaning and maintenance; 35% of workers in
construction and extraction; 27.3% of food preparation
and serving workers and 23.9% of transport workers.

Fact 9: ¡Viva México!
Outside of Mexico, the biggest Mexican Independence
Day parade is celebrated in Los Angeles, California.

Fact 10: Time for a Spring Break!
Over half a million United States residents, most of
whom are university students, travel to Mexico for a
holiday during the break between the first and second
academic semesters; a tradition known as Spring Break.

"When I arrived in Sacromonte, I was just another 49er,
AD. Looking for a better life than the one I had in Sonora, in
Mexico. Hoping to find a land of freedom, opportunity and
plenty. Ready to start from scratch with the help of my brothers
and cousins and, of course, Rosa Feliz, my dear Rosa, my
Mexican Rose.

"But they wouldn't let us start anew, AD. We found gold quickly, good gold, of course, and lots of it, and we staked our claim, like you were supposed to. But they came, AD. The Anglos came and they killed my half-brother, JC, and they whipped me, and they hurt Rosa, and they took my gold and then we had nothing. So, we *had* to steal, AD. And so, we did, but only from the rich Anglos and only to live. Horses, mainly. And we set some of those horses free, AD, too.

"And we wanted to go back across the Altar and Colorado deserts, back to Sonora and the Rancho Tapizuelas. But we wanted to go back with money, you see, AD. Money we could help our people with and money to build a new school in El Salado, where I learned about the world, AD, as a boy.

"But that never happened, AD. They wanted people like me dead, you see. But it was Rosa Feliz who died. And I found the men who did it and I killed them and I stole from the other Anglos. And then I was a wanted man, AD, the most wanted man in California. So, I hid, in The American River Hotel, here in Miner's Haven.

"Years later, I met a wonderful Mexican girl and we married, AD. Her name was Gabriela and she was from Tamaulipas. And we had a daughter, AD, called Aurora, and Aurora believed her daddy was dead, when all the while he was living at the other end of a tunnel in a hotel room with no windows, right here in Miner's Haven, disguising himself as an old man every weekend to trick the rich Anglos in the saloon out of their gold playing Three Card Monte so she and Gabriela had enough money to have a decent life, and pretending to be Gabriela's friend.

"They all knew who I was, AD. Everyone in Miner's Haven, except Aurora. But for some reason, nobody ever betrayed me. Maybe that was because Gabriela learned how to cure almost every illness with medicines from the plants that grew along the

2 **to stake your claim** to show that you are interested in sth (originally by putting a piece of wood in the ground to show that it is taken)

American River from her friend A`wa`y, a Chumash woman, and she helped everyone here stay healthy."

You think of your mom and the herbal medicine remedies she believes in and gives to people she cares about. You love her for that, you realize, and suddenly feel like crying.

You don't.

"Meeting you has made me happy, AD. Follow your dreams and the Universe will help you. Enter room 85. A treasure is waiting for you."

The desert disappears from the corridor walls and natural light enters through the high window again.

Your eyes adjust to the light.

You check your cellphone: still no network signal, still none of the Apps work. The time is twenty to two. And, inexplicably, the battery charge is now at 25%.

You approach the door to room number 85. You try the handle, the door opens, and you step inside.

The door closes behind you.

The first thing you notice is that there is a clock that has no glass.

The clock has stopped at five o'clock.

The bed in the room is identical to the one in the previous room. There is a fireplace and a dressing table. Light comes from a circular skylight. There's a wooden chair by the dressing table.

You sit down on the dressing table chair and open the draw in the table. Inside is a scrapbook.

On the first right-hand page of the scrapbook there is an illustration of a primitive fishhook. Under this illustration there is a description of the hook, but a strip of paper containing the top halves of the letters in the first sentence of the description is missing.

I purchased this for 2 cents from a Pomo Indian begging

On the next six right-hand pages of the scrapbook, there are also texts describing primitive fishhooks, all with strips of paper with the top halves of the letters in the first sentence of the description missing, and with a space above these texts for illustrations that, presumably, the owner of the scrapbook didn't have time to do.

You look at yourself in the dressing table mirror, waiting for a message to appear.

Nothing happens.

You stand up and take the letter to Joaquín Murrieta from your pocket and read it in search of an explanation of what's happening to you.

You find none.

You look at the map your father drew and wonder where he and your mom and your brothers and sister are now. They probably haven't missed you yet and, knowing Selena, have gone to check out McQueen's Store, where miners were probably enthusiastically "mined" for dollars in return for mining utensils.

You, you decide, are in The American River Hotel.

There's still no cellphone network coverage, and your battery charge is now at 12%.

You stand up again, not knowing what to do. Then you see that the strips of paper missing from the scrapbook have been pasted onto the back of the door.

You remove all the strips of paper from the door and sit down again at the table.

You open the scrap book again.

> ## Listen to the clue!

---

15 **enthusiastically** done with lots of excitement and passion

You manage to match seven of the drawings to their pages then, not really understanding what you're achieving by doing so, you match the last three.

Karok hook, carved from bone. Found in 1852
near the Klamath River, Oregon.
The Karok probably used it to fish for trout, which are
abundant in the area.
Bought for 1 dollar.

J.T.
April 20, 1850

Purchased from a Pomo Indian beggar

Karok hook carved from bone. Found in 1852

Bought by he who writes from a Chamush
elder I encountred on Limuw Island in 1845,
it still retains the tar with which it would have been attached
to the piece of hemp string the Chamush used to fish with.
It is carved on abalone shell. Paid 2 dollars.
Beautiful.

J.T.
March 4, 1850

Bought by he who writes from a Chamush

Purchased from a Pomo Indian beggar,
on Dupont Street, San Francisco.
Unusual, as the Pomo Indians normally
used baskets to collect their fish.
Cost me 2 cents.

J.T.
May 6, 1850

When you slide the last strip of paper into place, you hear the voice of the girl coming from the other side of the room door, only, as Joaquín Murrieta was, the girl is older now.

"What is the largest number you can see in the last three scrapbook entries, AD?" she asks.

Your cellphone begins to vibrate again and you hear the same heavy footsteps from the room above as in Murrieta's real hideaway.

> **DANGER!**

flashes on your cellphone screen and the battery charge is at 2%.

You look at the description of the fishhook J.T. (James Thomas, presumably) paid for.

"Now double the first two digits, for example, 17 would be 34. Then multiply the last two digits, for example, 22 would be 4. Then multiply this by 2. Add the two results, for example, 1722 would be 42," says the young woman's voice.

Your phone is now vibrating frantically and the footsteps in the room above you are getting more and more agitated.

You find the date the young woman mentions, do the Math she explains and say _____.

You hear a "click" and the room door opens slightly. You look at your cellphone, which has stopped vibrating. The battery charge has gone up to 22% but nothing on it is working. You put the phone, Murrieta's letter and your dad's map of Miner's Haven in your trouser back pockets and leave the room.

There is nobody in the corridor

The room door closes behind you.

🔓 Immediately, you look for door _____.

For want of a nail ...

When you have escaped this chapter, check your answers to these questions by looking at the answer key on page 156.

Do you know what the thirteen stripes on the United States flag represent?

The thirteen colonies that declared independence from Great Britain, in 1776.	
The first thirteen articles of the U.S. constitution.	
13 May, 1776, when U.S. independence was claimed.	
The 13 biggest cities in the U.S.	

What do you think this is?

Test your general knowledge

This chapter includes a popular poem in English. Can you complete it?

For want of a nail, the shoe was lost.
For want of a _____, the horse was lost.
For want of a _____, the rider was lost.
For want of a _____, the battle was lost.
For want of a _____, the kingdom was lost.
And all for the want of a horseshoe _____.

Useful words and expressions

Knowing the meaning of these words will help you escape from this chapter.

Embroidery is decorative craft used to make pictures with thread.
A motto is a short sentence, sometimes in Latin, that expresses the spirit of an organisation.
A fool is a person who is not very intelligent and who makes simple errors.
A quilt cover is a sort of large, cloth envelope, often made from different squares of cloth, that we put a quilt in to keep it clean while we sleep under it.

Talking point

The most important object in this chapter is a journal. Have you ever kept a journal? What type of things did you write in it? What types of things do you think would be in AD's journal? Talk to your classmates and share your ideas.

You walk up to each of the remaining doors in the corridor and try to memorize each door number, 27, 32, 54, 101, 154. That way, you've decided, it will be easier to get out of room 97, as you'll be able to recognize the possible correct numbers in the challenge you face in there.

Just as you start making your way towards room 97, the high window at the end of the corridor goes dark and images on the walls either side of you and on the ceiling above and on the floor beneath make you feel like you're floating in space, falling towards planet Earth, through a rainbow, towards the ocean, where you're surrounded by dolphins.

Then the corridor goes totally dark.

You hear 'A`wa`y's voice but cannot see her in the corridor.

"The Chumash believe that Hutash, the Earth Mother, created people by planting the seeds of a magical plant on Limuw Island, AD. We believe the first Chumash grew from the ground.

"Then Hutash saw that we were cold and asked her husband, Alchupo'osh, the Sky Snake, or the Milky Way, to help. So Alchupo'osh used his tongue to send a bolt of lightning which started a fire on Limuw and the Chumash kept the fire alive.

"But there were soon too many Chumash for the island and there were so many of us that the sound of people singing and dancing and of children laughing and crying at night stopped Hutash from sleeping.

"So, Hutash decided to make a bridge from Limuw Island to the mainland so the Chumash could populate new lands and she made the bridge from a rainbow, which we call a wishtoyo, and it went from a mountain on Limuw Island to a mountain on the mainland, where she had made sure there was plenty of wonderful places to live and lots of food.

"Hutash told the people to only look forward when they were on the rainbow bridge, never down, because the bridge was high and they might lose their balance and fall. But on the bridge, some people looked back at Limuw, or looked down, and lost their balance, and fell towards the ocean and feared they would die.

"But they didn't, AD, Hutash changed the people who fell from the rainbow bridge into dolphins, you see.

"Perhaps they were the lucky ones."

Light fills the corridor again.

You open the door to room 97 and enter.

The door closes behind you.

The room you find yourself in is filled with the daylight entering through an open window.

The room shows no signs of the passage of time and smells of pine incense.

The iron frame of the bed appears to have been recently painted. On the dressing table, there are two flasks of perfume, what looks like a journal, a woman's fan, open and showing an image of the warship the USS Constitution, perhaps, after The Mayflower, the most famous ship in History, now moored in Charleston, Boston, you seem to remember from some "History Day" or other, with your family.

There's a chandelier fixed to the ceiling above the bed, with four unlit candles. A square of luxurious carpet covers the floor next to to bed and its dark, light green color compliments the lime-colored, damask wallpaper decorated with a fleur-de-lis pattern that covers every inch of wall, except the fireplace.

The chair at the bedside table is padded and covered with blue velvet, and there's a wash table with a bowl in which the water is still warm.

And there's a wardrobe similar to the one in Uwe Dresler's room. You approach it and open it. The air inside smells of lavender. Thirteen woman's dresses, all black, are hanging from the rail: the room was clearly the reside of a widow.

There are four flower pressings hanging from the wall opposite the bed.

You look at the pressings and at the embroidery sample hanging on same wall.

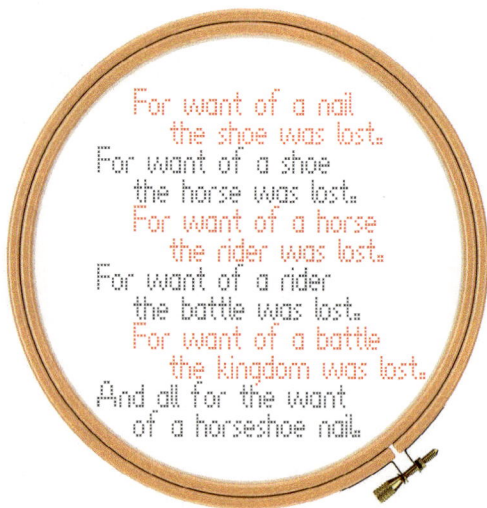

For want of a nail
    the shoe was lost.
For want of a shoe
    the horse was lost.
For want of a horse
    the rider was lost.
For want of a rider
    the battle was lost.
For want of a battle
    the kingdom was lost.
And all for the want
    of a horseshoe nail.

---

15 **embroidery** artwork created with stitching on material

102

It's a sort of poem, that your mom sometimes says to you and Selena and Jake and Elmore when she thinks you haven't prepared properly for whatever challenge you're about to face.

10 FUN FACTS ABOUT
THE ROLE OF WOMEN
IN THE CALIFORNIAN GOLD RUSH

Fact 1: At first, very few women participated in the Californian Gold Rush.
According to the 1850 Census of California, only 8% of the population in California was female.

Fact 2: Changes in the role of women happened back home.
When many brave women started to leave their homes across America to travel to the goldfields, traditional communities began to consider the role of women in American life in a new light.

Fact 3: Many women made lots more money than at home.
The traditional, poorly-paid jobs the women who travelled to California did were much better paid in the gold towns than they were at home. This helped these women become more independent and, in some cases, rich.

Fact 4: Looking after the family financially

When women travelled to the gold fields with their husbands and families, often the husband had no luck finding gold and it was their wives that made sure the family was okay.

Fact 5: Women writers

One of the best descriptions of life during the Gold Rush is *The Shirley Letters*, written by Louise Amelia Knapp Smith Clappe. Eventually, in 2017, the story these letters tell became an opera!

Fact 6: Legal freedom

Under Californian law, divorce for women was easier than in other parts of the United States. In fact, in 1850 more than 70 percent of all requests for divorce in California were made by women.

Fact 7: The male obsession with finding gold meant more opportunities for women.

Many women learned new skills during the Californian Gold Rush, as the men at the time were obsessed with finding gold. This process contributed to the slow emancipation of women.

Fact 8: The entertainment industry

Miners with lots of extra money paid lots of money to see women actors, dancers and singers perform on stage and many performers, such as Lotta Crabtree, became rich, independent women this way.

Fact 9: The battle for women's rights was accelerated.

Perhaps more than anywhere in the United States at the time, successful businesswomen during the Gold Rush helped demonstrate that women were just as capable as men at creating extremely successful companies, a fact that helped make people think twice about the role of women in society.

Fact 10: Non-Anglo women still had a difficult time.

Some historians say it was women from the Miwok tribe who taught early miners to use baskets to find gold in river sand. Unfortunately, at the time these women had no rights and would have none for many decades to come.

Finally, you take the matches and your cellphone from the back pockets of your pants and sit at the dressing table.

You open the drawer in the table.

Inside is an embroidery sampler, turned upside down, and a leather-bound journal.

You take both out of the drawer and put them on the table.

You turn the sampler over and see that it represents the original motto of the United States, "*E Pluribus Unum*".

You remember it means "Out of many, One."

You open the journal at the first page.

Only one day has been written about, Tuesday, 13 June, 1854.

You read what has been written.

Tuesday, May thirteen, 1854
Miner's Haven
Sacramento

Last night, Saul Gregson, a fellow guest, and I enjoyed a cup of tea whilst he read to me from the manuscript of the book he is compiling about the flowers and trees of Northern California and he graciously allowed me to give him my opinion on his progress.

Then he told me about his arrival at The American River and though I can't remember exactly what he said, it was something like this:

'We hired an ox team in Sacramento to carry our baggage and started for this place. We walked by the wagon and at night cooked our suppers, rolled our blankets

---

21 **to compile** to create – 22 **graciously** kindly – 31 **supper** evening meal

around us and lay down to rest on the ground, with nothing but the broad canopy of the heavens over us. When we arrived at Miner's Haven, we pitched our tents and slept again.

'The next day, we shouldered our picks and shovels and with pan in hand went to try our fortunes at gold digging. We did not have very good success, being green at mining, but by practice and observation we soon improved some, and found a little gold.'

Today is April thirteen. By chance a few days ago, to calm my nerves, I started working on a sampler of our motto: E Pluribus Unum and finished it this afternoon.

I must admit I intensely dislike the number thirteen. Does that make me no better than a pagan, like Mona, my son's "wife"? Thirteen letters like the thirteen founder states of our great country, thirteen years between me and ...

But that is not what matters, the age difference. Despite his calm, quiet side, Saul is a mere gold-digger and I cannot tell if he is after what's left of my husband's inheritance.

Yet I am so happy to see him, whenever ...

Stop right there, Sarah! Mona must surely need help with dinner for the permanent guests at the hotel.

---

3 **canopy** covering – 6 **pick** tool for mining – 6 **shovel** tool for mining – 17 **pagan** not religious – 26 **inheritance** money and land that sb leaves to sb else when they die

This is not the time to let yourself be fooled by thoughts of romance. Even though this evening, over tea, you caught yourself falling in love with a gold-digging flower collector, who, for the last few weeks has made your heart sing again with his beautiful flower pressings.

In that respect, James is more like me than his father, may God rest his soul. James too is a romantic fool, ready to fall for even an uneducated, superstitious Indian girl!

Remember, what day of the month it is today, Sarah Thomas.

It's the day in April 2 years ago when James announced he was leaving Boston; the day in July, 7 years ago when his father died; the number of founding states of this crazy nation; the number of times you say to yourself every night that you shall not fall in love with a gold-digging flower collector named Saul Gregson!

You examine the embroidery sample, check that there are thirteen letters in your country's original motto, *E Pluribus Unum*, as well as thirteen red stripes in the original US flag, say to yourself, "Very Wowza" and smile as you remember Jake and Elmore.

And then, as if she were behind you, you hear the voice of `A`wa`y.

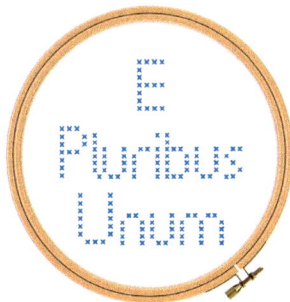

---

10 **superstitious** believing in old ideas about luck

"Sarah Thomas did fall in love with Saul Gregson, AD, of course" she says, mischieviously. "And he treated her right."

Your phone has not started vibrating, so you don't look at it, and there are no footsteps in the room above. Instead, you feel the presence of love in your heart, as if a grandmother had just given you a handmade present, a quilt cover, perhaps, that she'd spent months making for you.

"Sarah wrote the same number in letters several times in her journal entry, AD. Multiply that number by the number of times it appears and then subtract one from the result."

You look at the letter again and do what `A`wa`y says, while you try, and fail, to remember the door numbers you tried to memorize earlier.

"Say the number, AD."

🔓 You say _____ and the room door opens.

You consider leaving the box of matches, the letter from Murrieta's brother and the map your father gave you in the room, as they no longer seem to be of any use.

Then, in your head, you hear your mother's voice, saying: "For want of a nail …," so you leave everything in your pockets and walk towards the open door of the room.

🔍 **Listen to the clue!** 📖

---

6 **quilt** a kind of bed cover

Shot like a dog, by a dog

When you've escaped this chapter, check your answers to these questions by looking at the answer key on page 156.

Can you guess what these words in Chumash mean: "Mi sumi lho"?

I'm hungry.	
I live here.	
I love you.	
I am tired.	
Thank you.	

Do you know the word for these?

Test your general knowledge
The enigma in this chapter has to do with dice. Tick which of these statements about dice is true.
a. The earliest dice found are from Iran.
b. Dice is the plural form of die.
c. Opposite sides on a die add up to 8.
d. The name of the dots on a die is "pips".
e. When you roll two dice, seven is the most common result.

Useful words and expressions

Knowing the meaning of these words will help you escape from this chapter.

A person who is deaf and dumb cannot hear or speak.

A settlement is a place where people who are new to a wild place build houses.

A birthmark is a mark on a person's skin that is with them from when they are born.

To be delirious is to see and say strange things, often because you have a fever.

Talking point

In this chapter, a man tells AD that "We are all just stories, telling stories". What do you think he meant? Talk to your classmates, friends or family and share your ideas and experiences.

"Come close, AD."

`A`wa`y's voice seems to be coming from the opposite end of the corridor to the high window and is as quiet as a whisper.

You notice that the room numbers in the corridor have changed again.

"Come close, AD."

You obey.

"They were a wonderful person, AD, Pin and Yin became great friends of James and I. I showed them Chumash medicine and they showed me their Chinese remedies. Eventually, they married a deaf and dumb woman from Illinois and had children, two sets of non-Siamese twins."

A warm feeling washes over you when the high corridor window darkens and you see an image of Pinyin and his wife with two sets of happy twins.

"They were happy for a few years and sadly died young, as Siamese twins so often did in those days.

DID YOU KNOW? 10 FUN FACTS ABOUT THE ROLE OF THE CHINESE IN THE CALIFORNIA GOLD RUSH

Fact 1: They were motivated by poverty.
In the early 1800s, many people, especially in Southern China, were poor. One solution was for families to pay for brothers and sons to travel to the Californian Gold Rush.

Fact 2: They had a considerable presence in California.
In 1852, 20,000 Chinese people arrived in California. This was approximately 30 percent of all immigrants who arrived that year.

Fact 3: Most Chinese immigrants sent money home.
When Chinese immigrants made money either through mining for gold or earning wages doing other jobs, they usually sent some home. This improved their families' lives.

Fact 4: They were very patient.
Chinese miners often occupied gold mines abandoned by Anglos who didn't have the patience to continue looking for gold at these mines and preferred to look for new places to mine. However, these mines often contained substantial quantities of gold.

Fact 5: They knew about water.
Many Chinese immigrants had worked as farmers back in China and so were very good at working in and with water to find gold. Water and irrigation techniques, of course, were, and are still, essential to Chinese rice farming.

Fact 6: Chinese gold diggers were very flexible.
One of the characteristics of early Chinese gold miners was that they used simple tools to extract gold. This meant they could move from one place where there was gold to another very quickly.

Fact 7: They had no rights.

Californian law in 1849 said, 'No Black, or Mulatto person, or Indian shall be allowed to give evidence in favor of, or against a White man' and Chinese people were included in this group of people. For this reason, many innocent Chinese people were found guilty of crimes they didn't commit and were executed.

Fact 8: Personae non gratae

Towards the end of the Californian Gold Rush, when finding gold became more difficult, Chinese miners faced more aggression from Anglo miners who simply claimed Chinese gold mining places for themselves.

Fact 9: They started communities.

The famous Chinatown area of San Francisco is the oldest Chinese community in the United States and was established during the California Gold Rush.

Fact 10: The Chinese brought new spiritual practices to the United States.

None of the main Chinese religions, Confucianism, Buddhism or Taoism, were common in the United States, but helped the Chinese immigrant miners who arrived during the Gold Rush to survive the difficulties they encountered.

"Can I take you back to the four or five days that James and I got to know each other, AD; the days when we learned so much from and about each other and fell irreversibly in love?"

"Yes," you reply.

Light returns to the corridor and the sound of the Pacific Ocean waves washing over a beach fills your ears.

"Thank you. It was summer and at night, James slept under the stars, wrapped in a warm blanket, within sight of his tent, where I slept.

---

26 **irreversibly** impossible to change

"Those first few days were spent telling each other our life stories. And not just the events that our lives had contained, AD. We talked about our dreams, fears, ambitions, wishes, hopes, successes and disappointments.

"James had arrived in New York five years earlier after spending his childhood and youth in a country called Wales, which I had never heard of, where he had trained to be a dentist. Then, in Boston, he had set up a dental practice and had been reasonably successful.

"But his real passion, AD, was for American History. Not the history that began in 1620, when the Pilgrim fathers alighted from The Mayflower in Plymouth Bay, mind you. James wanted to know about the history of the people who had lived here for over twenty thousand years before that, and he came to California in the Gold Rush not only to look for gold, though he did that too, and well, but to talk to the Native Americans he knew would be mistreated, derided and flung into despair because of the arrival of people from all over the world. He also wanted to talk about the diseases these people would bring with them and the disrespect with which the Anglos regarded thousands of years of Native American culture. Three hundred thousand gold-diggers arrived in California between 1848 and 1852, AD; imagine that!

"And I told James everything, AD. And after every sentence of mine, AD, I expected him to judge me, but he didn't. Not even once.

"I told him about the village where I used to live, before Shu`nu decided to take us to the gold fields, where every autumn we would collect the acorns Hutash put on the oak trees and store them for the whole year. I told him about my brothers and sisters and my cousins and grandparents and aunts and uncles and he

---

11 **to alight from** to get off a ship – 17 **to mistreat** to treat badly – 17 **to deride** to humiliate – 17 **to fling into despair** to make very upset – 29 **acorn** a kind of nut that comes from an oak tree

wrote the names of them all down in his notebook and asked me
to teach him how to pronounce them.

"He asked me what we ate and how we greeted each other
in the morning and said goodnight. He asked us about our
weddings and funerals and games and travels and contacts with
other Indians who were not Chumash. He asked me how to say "I
love you" in my language and I told him: 'Mi sumi lho.'

"And then one day, when I woke up in his tent, I went to look
for him in the place he slept, under his blanket, and the blanket
was there, but he wasn't, so I went to look for his boat and it was
where it always was, but again, he wasn't there, and I realized I
didn't want to be separated from him, ever. And when I went
back to where his blanket was, I found him, but he was ill with
stomach cramps, so I went to look for the plants I would need
to make him an infusion and a few hours after drinking it, the
stomach cramps had gone though he still had a fever, so I helped
him back to his tent, out of the sun, and I gave him some more
of the infusion and he fell asleep and I lay down beside him and
in his sleep he said, 'Mi sumi lho,' and laughed. Then he said, 'Mi
sumi lho, `A`wa`y.'

"The next day James was better and said we should go.

"'Where to?' I asked and he explained that he needed to go
to San Francisco for money and then, he suggested, we would
leave the boat there, or sell it, and make our way back to Miner's
Haven, to my family.

"So, we did. We sailed to San Francisco, but we couldn't sell the
boat, because nobody wanted to go to sea anymore, everybody
who arrived in San Francisco wanted to go straight to the
goldfields, you see, so James picked up his money from Boston
and we decided to stay for three nights in San Francisco before
heading inland."

---

31 **to head inland** to move away from the coast

Suddenly the corridor fills with the sights and sounds of San Francisco at the start of the Gold Rush, as if it were a passageway running between ramshackle, wooden buildings.

"And then, AD, James proposed marriage to me and I said yes, because my heart told me to, and a judge married us in San Francisco. James gave me a Welsh love spoon he'd made himself in secret and a ring with the words *Mi sumi lho* engraved on the inside of it. After two nights in separate hotel rooms, we spent the last night in just one, and the next day we bought a horse and trap and we set off for Miner's Haven. It took us two weeks because we would stop along the way, whenever James saw signs of an Indian settlement, or we came across Indian people. James would ask the people in these villages, or solitary travelers, where they were going and from where they had come and he would write everything he learned about them down. But not only the Indians, AD, he talked to the Chinese, the Europeans, the people from Hawaii, the people from Mexico and South America. And sometimes I would help them with one of my maternal grandmother's herbal remedies and they would want to pay us, but we would refuse.

"And he explained a theory to me, AD. He said that my people came from Mongolia, which was near China. He explained that one day somebody would prove that people from Mongolia had followed mammoths across the North Pole when the ocean there was frozen and that they had then walked south to Limuw Island and even down to near the South Pole, and founded villages along the way, and that the clue to the fact that this was true was the birthmark Native Indians in every country in America and babies from Mongolia were all born with at the base of their spine. And he called me Mona, a name people who spoke Old English gave to the Moon, he told me."

---

3 **ramshackle** rundown

In the corridor, San Francisco still surrounds you, but night has fallen.

"It's getting late, AD, and it is your birthday after all. I shall be brief.

"James and I eventually made it to the outskirts of Miner's Haven and camped. James rode on, determined to find out who the Anglo gold-digger who had made Shu`nu scribble something on a contract was. He paid the Anglo so that my father was no longer obliged to work for the man all day seven days a week.

"At first, my mother wouldn't speak to me, and my father just asked me 'why?'"

Suddenly, a man, carrying prospector's equipment emerges from corridor wall to your right and crosses the corridor, stops to look straight at you and says, "Oliver Laidlaw, pleased to meet you. Nobody is really where they think they're from, by the way. Nobody. We are all just stories, telling stories."

The man disappears into the opposite wall of the corridor.

"First, we built a shack," continues `A`wa`y. "And James panned for and found lots of gold. Then, he told me he had enough money to build something bigger, where Shu`nu and Leqte could work and make money and that he had found an investor, a French gold assayer. That 'something bigger' was this hotel, AD, and when it was finished we kept one floor for people who lived here all year round, while the rooms upstairs were for guests who only stayed a few days.

"Eventually, my parents accepted James as a son-in-law, AD. But only after he had drunk the drink Chumash boys had to when they were eight, *moymoy*, made from datura, or moonflower, that takes you to hell, and back, if you are lucky, and which prepared a boy, my people believed, to be a warrior, if necessary.

"Eventually, our three children were born and when our parents died we all went to Europe, and James taught Native American History in universities in London and Paris and my sister ran The American Hotel, until folk stopped mining for gold near Miner's Haven and everybody left.

"It was James' idea that your great-great-great-great-grandfather, Joaquín Murrieta come here with Gabriela and Aurora, AD, after he came across them in a cave one winter's day, half-frozen, but with enough gold to buy a palace: gold that was absolutely no good at all to them …

"He was a good man, AD."

Silence.

You open the door to room 109. Broken in several places, the window shutters offer some light and you see that the only furniture in the room is a wooden chair and a table with a green poker tablecloth on it and ten dice.

You remove your cellphone from one of your back pockets to take a picture, but no longer feel anxious that there is no coverage, no functionality and that the battery charge is 5%.

Instead, you take the box of matches from your other back pocket and you sit down.

Then the voices in the room begin.

"He's delirious Gabriela," you hear `A`wa`y say.

You remember that Gabriela was Joaquín Murrieta's second wife.

"Do you want me to have Joaquín send one of his men for the doctor?" replies a young woman's voice with a pronounced Mexican accent.

27 **delirious** mad, crazy

"There's no time," answers A`wa`y.

Then it's a man's weak voice you hear, which seems to emerge from a place between where A`wa`y and Gabriela are sat; as if there were a bed between the women and the man was lying on it, being attended to by the two women.

"It was going so well Blanche," mumbles the man, though there seems to be no such person as Blanche in the room. "So well. I was living in a cabin with six other miners, including your brother, Nathan. There were glass windows, Blanche, a fireplace and an oven. Come closer, Blanche, my love. Please."

The man's accent, you believe, reveals he is from The East Coast.

"He thinks *you're* Blanche, Gabriela," says `A`wa`y.

"Our diet was poor though, Blanche," continues the man, struggling to speak. "So poor, and I had scurvy for a while and then fever, but I got better. So many that come here looking for gold meet with disaster, Blanche, and thousands will leave their bones here. Others will lose their health, contract diseases that they will carry to their graves with them. Some will have to beg their way home, and probably one half that come here will never make enough to carry them back. We are such poor, frail beings, my love."

"I shall go for water," says `A`wa`y. You hear the door to the room open and close and the sound of `A`wa`y's footsteps growing fainter.

"Oh, Blanche," the man continues, "Hold my hand. Thank you. There is so much sin and wickedness in the gold fields. Stealing and lying and swearing and drinking and every saloon is a place for gambling and men win and lose thousands of dollars in a night and even small boys bet five or ten dollars and if they lose everything, go out the next day and dig alongside the men."

---

15 **scurvy** an illness caused by not getting enough vitamin C – 27 **sin** bad behavior –
27 **wickedness** bad behavior – 29 **to gamble** to put money on the outcome of sth (usually sport results)

Then there is silence until you hear `A`wa`y returning and opening and closing the door into the room.

"I'm dying Blanche. Shot like a dog, by a dog. I had never played dice before, Blanche. But I had a good day today on the gold fields. Wanted to live a little, I suppose. And I was winning, Blanche, and had decided to leave the saloon, but they wouldn't let me, Blanche, the two men from the North. They wouldn't let me. But I left anyway, with three thousand dollars, and decided to spend the night, just one, in the hotel. I felt the pain in my back before I heard the gunshot, Blanchy, and for a moment was more worried about my nose, which I feared broken from when I hit the ground, than I was about the bullet in my back. And they took the money, Blanche. And I didn't see who."

"Sh," you hear `A`wa`y say. "Don't get agitated, Robert. You must rest."

"No, Blanche, no. I will be gone soon and will never hold you or my darling John and Michael up to the sky or carry you on my back again."

You hear a man's footsteps in the corridor.

You hear the door into the room open.

"Will he survive?" whispers Joaquín Murrieta.

"Father?" says the dying man. "Is that you father? Forgive me, father. Forgive me."

"I forgive you, son," says Murrieta.

Then Murrieta whispers: "My men have found the two who did it, Gabriela. We did not hurt them, but we will make sure Robert's money gets to his family."

The room door closes again.

"I'm on the banks of the river now, Blanche," continues the dying man. "On the banks of The American River. The *great* American River. And it's beautiful, Blanche and there are other people on the banks too, for as far as I can see, on either side.

---

14 **to get agitated** to get upset

Men mostly. Tarheads, greasers, men from Hawaii, Chile,
Ecuador, Peru, Canada, France, Germany. There are even black
men, Blanche, and there are Indians: the Chumash, the Alliklik,
the Kitanemuk, the Serrano, the Kumeyaay, the Karok and the
Pomo, Blanche, all holding pans, ready to wade into the water
and find gold, but not for themselves, for their masters. And their
hope never dies, Blanche, because the river water washes that
hope clean, every day, Blanche, every single day!"

Silence.

"`A`wa`y," says Gabriela.

"It all goes back to the river, Blanche ...." says the dying man.

You hear a man's footsteps in the corridor and the door
opening. The man enters.

"He's gone, Nathan," says `A`wa`y.

You hear the man leave the room, close the door and walk
away.

Then you hear Gabriela and `A`wa`y leaving, too.

Silence.

"There are letters scored into the dice, AD."

Your blood chills: it is the dead man, Robert's, voice you hear.

"The letters make a two-digit number."

Silence.

You examine the dice and see that there are indeed lines scored into them. You turn the faces these lines have been drawn on towards you on the tabletop.

You strike a match and blow it out, take the map of Miner's Haven your dad gave you and turn it over. Then you draw ten squares on it.

When you finish writing the letters in the squares, nothing happens.

"Put the actual dice in order, AD," says the dead man's voice and you obey.

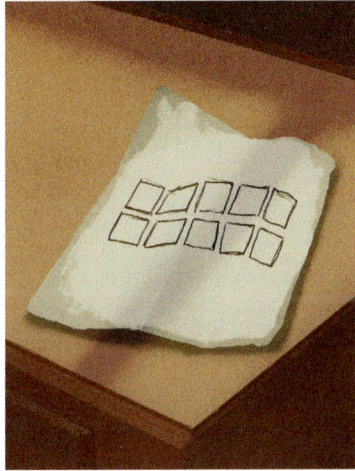

When you've made the number _____, the room door clicks open.

Listen to the clue!

Hocus pocus

When you've escaped this chapter, check your answers to these questions by looking at the answer key on page 156.

There are verb phrases in this chapter. Do you know what these mean?

to make sure that	to be positioned next to
to go up	to organize things so that something happens
to go down	to cease to exist, to end
to run out	to decrease
to stand by	to increase

Do you know what this skull is made from?

Test your general knowledge

In this chapter, Captain Harry Love uses the Spanish-Mexican expression *¡Hasta nunca!* Do you know what these expressions from other languages, but commonly used in English, mean?

a. Bon appetit!
b. Hey, presto!
c. cul-de-sac
d. Ciao!

Useful words and expressions

Knowing the meaning of these words will help you escape from this chapter.

A bounty was the amount of money the capturer wanted killer, or a criminal would receive.

To spit is to expel saliva from the mouth.

To take down is an informal way of saying "to kill."

Pretty can be used to mean "quite", as in "I'm pretty sure."

Talking point

In this chapter, Captain Harry Love says, "They're two intelligent ladies, Mr. Murrieta, Mona and Gabriela, especially for an Indian and a Mexican." Do you think it's appropriate to say that some nationalities or ethnic groups are more or less intelligent than others? Talk to your classmates, friends or family and share your ideas and experiences.

"Well done, AD! You solved the letter puzzle. Your ancestors are proud of you."

This time, the corridor window hasn't gone dark and A`wa`y is nowhere to be seen.

"Including me, little old A`wa`y. And Joaquín Murrieta. And Uwe Dresler, who married an Italian New Yorker, called Mina. And James Thomas, the Boston ethnographer who I fell in love with and married and still love today."

The voice of A`wa`y seems to be coming from under the floorboards.

"My husband, James, AD, and his mother managed this hotel for twenty years, until the gold ran out and nobody came here anymore."

You're not sure what to say, so you say nothing.

"I know that's probably hard for you to believe, AD, but it's true. Would you like to hear *my* story, AD? After all, it's your and your family's story, too."

Should you answer?

"AD, would you like to hear a little of my story?"

"Yes," you reply, surprised by the sound of your own voice.

Instinctively, you check your cell phone. Still no coverage. Still, none of the Apps work. 25% battery.

"AD, tell me what you know about the Chumash."

A few years ago, by boat, with your family, you visited Limuw Island, known as Santa Cruz Island since the arrival of the Spanish in 1602, then headed back to the mainland just as the sun was setting and your dad told you that the first film version of Peter Pan had been set on the island there, in 1924, and that you should all go see the film if it was ever shown at the beautiful California Theatre in San José, which it was, a year later.

You say: "The Chumash, you, are a Native Indian tribe, who used to fish. I think a lot of Chumash people died because of the

---

7 **ethnographer** sb who studies different cultures and their behavior

illnesses the outsiders brought with them from around the world, during the Gold Rush. I saw one of your villages in the tunnel. You were probably obliged by the settlers to work for them and lost your land, I guess."

5   "Not bad, AD, not bad at all. You've got a good memory."

Suddenly, an intricate pattern appears on each corridor wall, mirroring the pattern on the wall opposite.

"This was supposed to be how I spent my life, AD, weaving baskets for gold diggers. The Chumash are the best basket
10 weavers in the world, you see, AD. And that's what I was supposed to do. Marry a Chumash, weave baskets with juncus coiled so tight that the basket could hold water and be used for cooking and watch with resignation as first the Californianos took what they wanted from my people, then the rest of the folk
15 who came here looking to get rich did the same.

"Because, when I was nine, gold, lots of gold, was found inland, near Coloma, and my father decided to look for work along The American River and he made my mother and brother and sisters walk here from our village on the coast and he found work on a
20 placer's mine near here, except the 49ers didn't pay him. Or rather they did, but by giving him acorns that we could have found ourselves, just as we had done for ten thousand years, to make flour with. And Dad was tricked into becoming a slave and it broke his heart and he missed our village so much. We all did. And we would
25 talk about it every night in our tent, near the placer mine, while we dreamed of our 'ap, our traditional house, back home. And my father was lost then, AD, because he had ignored the advice given to him by the shaman in our old village, in the siliyik, the sacred house: "Don't help them take gold from the land, Shu`nu," that was
30 my father's name; it means sleepyhead. "Don't help the outsiders take our land's soul. The sky people will be angry with all the Chumash, Shu`nu."

---

11 **juncus** a kind of plant that usually grows by a river – 12 **coiled** circled tightly around –
13 **resignation** *(here)* acceptance

Suddenly, the sound of thunder and people screaming echoes around the corridor and the noise is so loud that you have to cover your ears.

When it stops, A`wa`y says sadly, "And Shu`nu was lost, AD. Lost."

The sound of thunder and screaming stops.

"Go into room 124, AD. I'll be there waiting for you. You must do what I say. Will you?"

Again, you feel intimidated by talking to the voice of someone you cannot see. Someone who says she's your ancestor ...

"Will you, AD?"

"Yes," you mumble.

As you begin opening the door of room 124, you suddenly feel hungry and you remember you've had nothing to eat since you stopped on Interstate 80 for Jake and Elmore to go to the bathroom and for Selena to buy a "Feeling Lazy On Interstate 80" fridge magnet, and, involuntarily, you suddenly remember the Sunday breakfasts your mom and dad prepare when you're not on one of their "History Day" excursions and see yourself in the yard at home again, sat at a table overflowing with delicious Mexican and German flavors, and surrounded by your family.

And you remember your dad teaching you to count and then you teaching Selena, Jake and Elmore to count by counting the number of red berries in a cluster on the Toyon plants at the bottom of the yard.

And there are chicken tamales with their corn plant leaf wrapping on the table, and *atole* (Mexican hot chocolate with cinnamon and cane sugar), chilaquiles and detox smoothie in a jug, for Selena, and *Zwiebelkuchen* and *Kartoffelpuffer*.

The yellow goldsturm, the deep pink crape myrtle flowers and the blue concha flowers your mom once planted in the yard are beautiful and you imagine drawing the whole scene.

The door into room 124 closes behind you.

---

9 **intimidated** scared – 17 **involuntarily** without wanting to – 24 **cluster** group

---

The first thing you notice is a candle set in a brass candle
holder in the middle of a wooden table.

The candle weakly illuminates the room, whose window is
boarded up from the outside.

The space on the tabletop next to the candle holder is covered
by acorns, which have had a face carved into them and a number
written. There's the same fireplace and chimney as in the other
rooms, but no bed, no dressing table, and no wardrobe. Two
wooden chairs, painted Mexican blue, stand by the table.

Suddenly, you hear the footsteps of two people outside in the
corridor. A woman's and a man's, it seems, by the sound they make.

Then you hear the room door handle being turned and the
door opening. You spin round to look, but the door into the
room is still closed.

"Joaquín Murrieta, Captain."

The voice is `A`wa`y's and she's in the room.

---

19 **to illuminate** to light up

"Harry Love," says a man's voice.

"*Bienvenido*," says the same voice you heard in the tunnel: the voice belonging to Joaquín Murrieta.

"Heard a lot about you, señor Murrieta."

You hear the door close and A`wa`y's footsteps in the corridor as she walks away.

The chair to the left of the table, as you look at it, moves away from the table and you jump with fright.

In an instant, the chair moves closer to the table again.

"They're two intelligent ladies, Mr. Murrieta, Mona and Gabriela, especially for an Indian and a Mexican."

You wait for Murrieta to reply.

"Joke, Mr. Murrieta, joke …" says Harry Love.

"And you're pretty smart for an Anglo, Captain," replies Murrieta.

Harry Love laughs unconvincingly and spits on the floor.

Silence.

"Correct me if I'm wrong, Captain Love," says Murrieta eventually. "One week ago, the Californian governor, John Bigler, created the group of men you lead, I forget their name."

You hear Harry Love spit on the floor again, then say, "The Californian State Rangers, Mr. Murrieta."

Silence.

"And what makes *you* the best choice of leader for these rangers, Captain."

"I fought against your people in the Mexican War, Murrieta; killed hundreds of you. Then I became a ranger, and a good one in Texas. Then I was Los Angeles Deputy Sheriff. And I'm the best bounty hunter in California."

"Correct me if I'm wrong, *mi capitán*, but I understand there's now a bounty on my head and those of Joaquín Valenzuela, Joaquín Botellier, Joaquín Carrillo y Joaquín Ocomorenia. Is that correct?"

"Sure is."

---

16 **unconvincingly** not sounding real

"And the bounty is?"

"One thousand dollars, but that'll go up. I'll make sure it does."

"How?"

"By running the clock down. I have three months to find you
and your men."

"They're not *my* men."

"I know, Mr. Murrieta."

Silence again.

You hear the sound of something heavy being placed on the table.

"The hand of three-fingered Jack, Mr. Murrieta?"

"Yes, Captain. God rest his soul."

A chill runs down your spine.

"What else do you need?" asks Murrieta.

"Nothing, señor Murrieta. I already have your head, in a barrel
of whiskey."

"Who's head is it?"

"A greaser we caught stealing horses. I took him down
personally."

"Is that where you will be *taking me down*, too, Captain?"

"That depends on how much you want to live, señor Murrieta."

"How much, Captain?"

"Eight thousand dollars."

Another spit on the floor.

"When?"

"July 25. A few days before the bounty limit runs out. The
governor will be nervous by then. You'll need to be seen in and
around Arroyo de Cantúa in the days leading up to your death."

"And that'll be the end of it?"

"That will be the end of it, señor Murrieta. You have my word."

"How many of you are there, Captain?"

"Twenty rangers, Mr. Murrieta."

"And the witnesses?"

"I'll take care of that, Mr. Murrieta. I have seventeen prepared."

---

27 **to lead up to** to be previous to

"And what will you do with the, my, head, Captain?"

"Take it to Stockton, first, and put it on show. Then, take it round the mining camps. Charge a dollar to see it. Maybe bring it here. Then I'll be gone too, Mr. Murrieta."

"Mona!" Murrieta suddenly raises his voice.

"Hey, what's going on?" says Captain Harry Love as his chair moves backwards.

"I need to be sure, Captain," says Murrieta. "I am a man of honor. Do not fear."

Harry Love's chair moves closer to the table again and you hear him sit down.

Then you hear A`wa`y's footsteps in the corridor and the door open.

"It's time, Mona."

10 FUN FACTS ABOUT FAMOUS REAL AND FICTIONAL OUTLAWS AND BOUNTY HUNTERS

Fact 1: Outlaws: the clue is in the name.
Originally, being called an outlaw meant that anyone could kill or capture you, because all legal protection had been taken away from you and you were *outside the law*.

Fact 2: Many outlaws were superstars.
Outlaws like Jesse James became folk heroes, even though they were often cruel and violent criminals.

Fact 3: The deaths of outlaws were often mysterious.
Even though the man who killed America's most famous bounty hunter at the time, Billy the Kid, proved he had shot and killed him, many people claimed that he had not in fact died and that the outlaw and the bounty hunter had made a pact because they were actually friends.

Fact 4: Outlaws often worked in groups.
The famous 1890's outlaw, Butch Cassidy, was part of a group of criminals called The Wild Bunch, which included: Elzy Lay, Kid Curry, The Tall Texan, Harry Tracy, Will Carver, Laura Bullion and Flat Nose Curry.

Fact 5: Some outlaws were women.
Perhaps the most famous was Belle Star and, in true outlaw style, there are at least four versions of how she died!

Fact 6: Bounty hunters: the clue is also in the name.
When somebody announced that the person who captured or killed an outlaw would be paid for doing so, the first question was, "How much is the bounty?" i.e., how much money would the bounty hunter make?

Fact 7: Bounty hunters today
Michelle Gomez is a modern-day cyber bounty hunter who combines different types of online public and private information sources to find fugitives from the law.

Fact 8: When bounty hunters worked together

Many of the techniques used by bounty hunters were adopted by Alan Pinkerton, the founder of Pinkerton's National Detective Agency, in 1855. This agency eventually became the most famous of its type in the world.

Fact 9: Bounty hunting: an old, old job

Charietto was an ancient who worked for the Romans. He worked along the Rhine river, especially near Trier, in the 4th Century, and is considered one of the first bounty hunters.

Fact 10: Famous fictional outlaws

Famous fictional outlaws include: Robin Hood, El Zorro, Han Solo and Natasha Romanoff.

A`wa`y's (or Mona's) footsteps approach the table and the carved acorns begin to move as if she were running her hands over them.

The acorns turn over and over and change places, seemingly infinitely.

Again, there is silence.

Then A`wa`y says: "The truth skulls say Captain Harry Love is not lying, Joaquín."

You hear A`wa`y's footsteps as she leaves the room.

"We have a deal, Captain," says Murrieta, when A`wa`y has gone.

"Hocus pocus," says Captain Love, before spitting on the floor again.

"Perhaps. Mona will give you the money on your way out."

Captain Love's chair moves away from the table and his footsteps move towards the door.

"You know I'll be watching you, don't you, Captain?"

Captain Harry Love stops and turns.

"I wouldn't expect anything less, Murrieta. *¡Hasta nunca!*"

Suddenly, all the acorns turn skull face side up, as if under the impulse of Murrieta's hands. Then the candle flame goes out, leaving you in darkness.

A few seconds later you hear Murrieta stand up and leave the room.

You take out your cellphone and turn the torch on. Before your eyes, your battery charge goes down from 10 to 2%. From the room above, you hear a horrifying woman's scream in the corridor just as your cellphone starts flashing the message:

DANGER!

You remember the box of matches you took from Murrieta's room and take it out of your back pocket. There is a skull on the front. You flip it over, and notice a number on the back.

You sit on the chair Joaquín Murrieta was sitting on, remove a match from the box, strike it and light the candle.

Having faced five challenges by now, the next one becomes immediately clear to you: you need to match the skull on the matchbox to one of the acorn skulls on the table. The number on that acorn will be the number on the door of the next room, you're pretty sure. But you could be wrong, maybe that would be too easy.

If only you could remember the numbers you've seen on the doors in the corridor, it would make your task much easier. You try, but can't, and make a mental note to memorize the remaining room numbers when you are in the corridor again.

You look closely at the carved acorns and the image of the skull on the matchbox.

You find the skull that looks most like the one on the matchbox. You can't help thinking that the number on the back of the matchbox might be relevant. But how? You look at the back of the matchbox again, and realize that there is more than just a number there. Now it's clear to you that the number must be _____.

With a smile on your face, you put the matchbox in your pocket and pick up the acorn that helped you solve the enigma.

As you do so, the room door opens with a click.

Listen to the clue!

Pinyin

When you've escaped this chapter, check your answers to these questions by looking at the answer key on page 156.

Guess who the main characters in this chapter are.

Look at this clue and see if you can guess what was special about the two main characters in this chapter.

The shirts in the wardrobe have two holes for necks, but the trousers only have two legs.	

What is the number shown on this abacus?

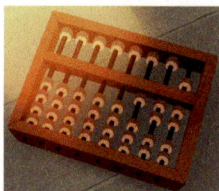

What do you know about murder ballads?

Murder ballads became very popular at the time of the California Gold Rush. Can you put these lines from a murder ballad in order? Write numbers.

Upon a frozen January day the dreadful deed was done;	
That happened near Fort Thomas in the old Kentucky State.	
She thought it was her husband's hand she could trust both night and day;	
They had been married but for one hundred and nine days.	
By Jackson and by Walling; how cold Pearl's blood did run!	
Young girls, if you'll listen, a story I'll relate;	

Useful words and expressions

Knowing the meaning of these words will help you escape from this chapter.

Something that is worthless has no value.

A ramshackle building is either badly constructed or has not been repaired for many years.

A slot is a long hole in an object into which you insert another object.

An indentation is an area on the surface of an object that is lower than the surface of the object.

Talking point

In the past, people would pay money to see unusual human phenomena such as very tall, or very small people. Why do you think that this is not the case today? Talk to your classmates, friends or family and share your ideas and experiences.

The first thing you do in the corridor is check the door numbers. They've changed again.

"Luckily for me and for my brothers and sisters," says 'A`wa`y, this time from your cellphone, which you take out of your back pocket, and now has 70% battery charge but no network coverage or functions, "there was a kind lady in the town, Mrs McQueen, who ran the store and who taught us how to count, just like your dad did with the toyon berries, and to read and write.

"That changed everything, AD. Thanks to Mrs. McQueen, by the age of eleven I had worked out how to read and did so whenever my chores allowed me to, until there were no more books in the village. And I tried to teach my mother and father to read too, AD, but they didn't want to learn. In fact, they hardly spoke any English, at all.

"Then my dad, Shu`nu, started drinking liquor after his fourteen-hour shifts for a placer who tricked him into becoming a slave. And he and my mom, Leqte, began to fight all the time and it got so bad that I ran away when I was seventeen and I wanted to go back to my people's home, to Limuw Island, where I hoped I would be beautiful, AD, because you see, I was convinced I was ugly, because that was how the settlers made us feel. Ugly and worthless, like cattle, AD."

The high window at the end of the corridor goes dark and the wall under it is filled with images of a teenage 'A`wa`y walking towards a ramshackle wooden shack, outside which her father, Shu`nu, is sat asleep, an empty bottle at his side.

"That's me AD.

"I had a little mirror that I found one day where people used to stack the rubbish."

The moving images you can see on the end wall of the corridor change and you see `A`wa`y and her brothers and sisters and mother sifting through a rubbish heap. `A`wa`y finds a piece of mirror but says nothing.

"And I would look in that mirror every day, AD, and see the same dumb, ugly Chumash girl looking back at me.

"Every single morning, evening and afternoon, for months, I saw the same me and didn't like her.

"Then I decided that the piece of the mirror was the problem, because it was old and cheap, I told myself, to reflect my image properly. So, the next time it rained, weeks later, I guess, I went in search of a puddle and, full of expectation, I stood over it and observed my reflection on the surface of the water.

"Of course, I saw the same me as ever. And the same thing happened when I walked all day to find a pool in The American River.

"Then I decided that the problem was that the water I was looking at myself wasn't deep enough. So, I spent another day walking to and back from Dark Lake. And I walked into the water, AD, as far as I could, with my eyes closed, and when I opened them, of course I saw the same `A`wa`y as always, only sadder.

"That day I ran away from Miner's Haven, AD.

"To the ocean.

"Because I'd decided that only by looking at myself in water as deep as the ocean would I ever know what I really looked like, who I really was.

"I walked for two weeks before I found myself on a beach.

"There were no boats to be seen: no Chumash tomols to take me out into the ocean, so I could see myself reflected on the surface of the deep ocean water. So I unrolled my blanket and slept and when I woke up, there was an Anglo, a little older than me, carrying a notebook and a small shovel, standing over me.

"'Good afternoon,' the Anglo said, and I was afraid, but didn't want it to show."

---

27 **to unroll** to make an object that has been made into a tube shape flat

"'Are you Chumash?'

I nodded and he smiled.

"'What's your name?'"

"'Mona,' I replied."

"'What's your real name?'"

I stood up and started to leave.

"'Wait,'" the Anglo said.

"He was handsome, AD, and seemed so kind.

"'I have a fire started near my boat and was going to cook some shellfish stew. Would you like some?'

"So, I said I would, which was true.

"And after being with this stranger, called James, from a place called Boston, and hearing his story, I dared to ask him to take me on his boat to Limuw Island and he agreed. And that afternoon, when we were halfway to Limuw, I asked him to stop the boat to see if any dolphins came (really I just wanted to look at my reflection in the calm, deep water). And he did stop the boat and I looked at my reflection on the surface of the sea and I saw the same old dumb, ugly `A`wa`y as ever and felt so sad, AD.

"But then, when I looked up from the water and into James Thomas' eyes, AD, I saw myself reflected in them and they were full of something strange and warm, and he smiled at me in a way I'd never been smiled at before, and he said, simply, 'You are beautiful `A`wa`y,' and then, for the first time since leaving our village for The American River in Sierra Nevada, in search of gold, I felt that I had come home."

"Now go into room 139, AD."

You obey.

As in Murrieta's room, there is no window. Nor is there a skylight. And when the room door closes, everything is in darkness.

You take the matches from your pocket and strike one.

There are eight candles in the room: two on the mantelpiece, two on the dressing table, whose chair is missing, and one on each corner of the bed frame. You light the candles.

On the dressing table there's a glass.

You go to the wardrobe and open it.

Inside there are beautifully sewn Chinese-style, silk shirts. You remove a shirt from its hanger and are intrigued to see that it has two neck holes. The rest of the shirts are the same.

You put the shirt back on its hanger and examine a pair of silk trousers. It has two legs.

Your cellphone begins to buzz. You look at it. You have 4% battery and the message now says:

HURRY UP AD!

19 **mantelpiece** the part of a fireplace where people place ornaments and other small objects

145

Then you notice an abacus,
on the floor near the bed,
marking the number 127.

A woman starts singing a
slow, sad song in the room
above you.

*Young girls, if you'll listen, a
story I'll relate;*

*That happened near Fort
Thomas in the old Kentucky State.*

Upon a frozen January day the dreadful deed was done;

By Jackson and by Walling; how cold Pearl's blood did run!

*She thought it was her husband's hand she could trust both night
and day;*

They had been married but for one hundred and nine days.

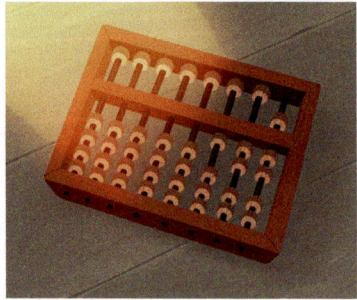

DID YOU KNOW?

10 FUN FACTS ABOUT THE ABACUS

Fact 1: When were abacuses first invented?
Nobody knows! The exact origin of the abacus is still a mystery.

Fact 2: The historical importance of abacuses
In 2013, the UNESCO declared the Chinese abacus as an
intangible cultural heritage element.

Fact 3: Heaven and earth
The top part of a Chinese abacus is called heaven and the
bottom part is called earth.

Fact 4: What do we call someone who uses an abacus?
The person who uses the abacus is called as abacist.

11 **deed** action

Fact 5: Abacus champions
Japanese pupils regularly take part in abacus local, regional and international abacus competitions.

Fact 6: A Chinese abacus allows the user to do hexadecimal computations, decimal computations, division, multiplication, getting square roots, and cube roots.

Fact 7: The Aztecs used a version of the abacus that used corn kernels instead of beads.

Fact 8: Still used today
Even today, people who work in commerce and administration in some parts of Eastern Europe, Russia, China, and Africa still use abacuses in their everyday work.

Fact 9: You don't need to see an abacus!
Many blind people also find abacuses extremely useful when doing complicated calculations.

Fact 10: What do you call more than one abacus?
There are two ways to form the plural of abacus: abacuses or abaci.

You kneel down by the abacus and wonder what to do with it. You sense it is your way out of the room.

The woman starts to repeat her murder ballad.

And this gives you the clue – you know what number you have to try. It works and the door clicks open.

You enter the hotel corridor.

Listen to the clue!

The door shuts behind you and the strange voice stops singing. You look for room ____.

Build your vocabulary

The American River – the mind map

Make your own mind map of words connected to the story.
Think of words to add to each topic area. You can add your own
topic areas too.

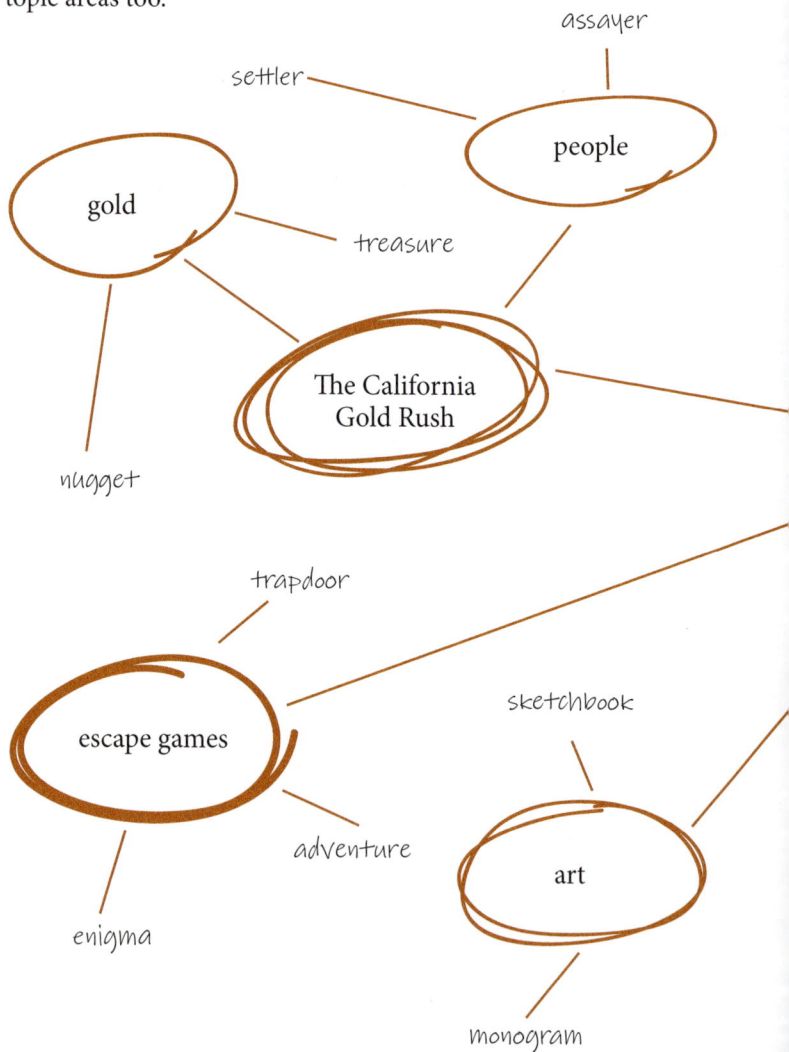

assayer

settler

people

gold

treasure

The California
Gold Rush

nugget

trapdoor

sketchbook

escape games

adventure

art

enigma

monogram

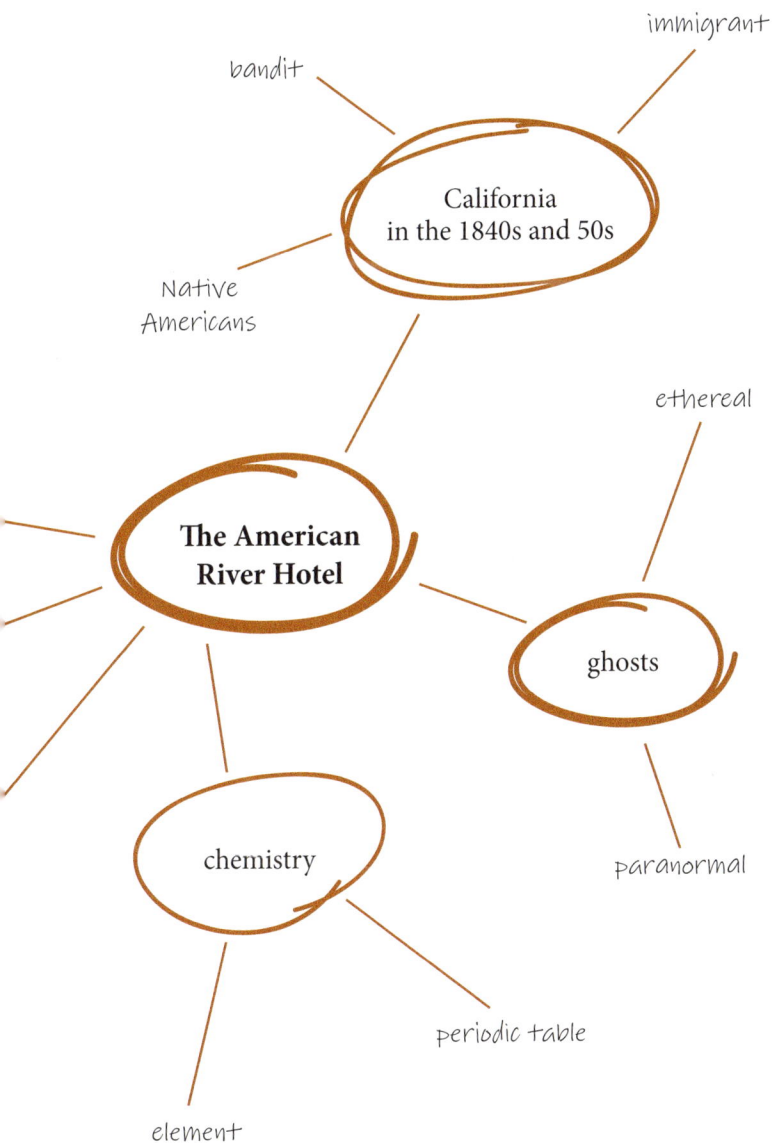

bandit

immigrant

California
in the 1840s and 50s

Native
Americans

ethereal

The American
River Hotel

ghosts

chemistry

paranormal

periodic table

element

Glossary

	New word?	Notes / connected words

The California Gold Rush

assay ☐
assayer ☐
extract ☐
gold digger ☐
gold fields ☐
indigenous tribe ☐
ingot ☐
long tom ☐
miner ☐
nugget ☐
pan ☐
pick ☐
prospector ☐
settler ☐
shovel ☐
strike it rich ☐
treasure ☐

Escape games

adventure ☐
combination lock ☐
device ☐
enigma ☐
experience ☐
explore a room ☐
keyhole ☐
secret door ☐
set up ☐
trapdoor ☐

California in the 1840s and 50s

bandit ☐
emigrate ☐
immigrant ☐
make your fortune ☐
Native Americans ☐
settlers ☐

Art

carbon dated ☐
monogram ☐
sketchbook ☐

Chemistry

chemical symbols ☐
element ☐
extinguish ☐
furnace ☐
melt ☐
molten gold ☐
periodic table ☐
purity ☐

Ghosts

ethereal ☐
ghost town ☐
paranormal ☐

🌐 **Find out more**

1. Choose one of the topics which are touched on in *The American River*. Find out more about it. Present your findings to your class, make a poster, or create a series of journal entries as AD.

The California Gold Rush

Albrecht Dürer

The American Dream

Joaquín Murrieta

Native Americans

the paranormal

settlers

immersive experiences

immigrants

2. What are immersive experiences? Have you had an immersive experience? What are the advantages and disadvantages of learning through an immersive experience?
   Find an example of an immersive experience on the internet. Tell your class about it.

Answer key

Sunday history trips

- AD, you; Selena Dresler, your sister; Rosa Murrieta Dresler, your mom; Jake and Elmore Dresler, your twin brothers; Karl Dresler, your dad.
- One half of a wooden number circle.
- 1. c.; 2. b.; 3. a.

You're a smart kid, AD

- True: He had a French accent.; He had a beard.; His office was in The American River Hotel.; He was a chemist.
- The periodic table.
- 1. b.; 2 a.; 3. b.

Murrieta's real hideaway

- True: He lived in The American River Hotel.
- A box of matches.
- 1. c.; 2. b.; 3. a.

It all goes back to the river

- 10.; Jean-Pierre Aurelian; Joaquín Murrieta's room; Jean-Pierre Aurelian's room; Somebody being shot, a baby crying, footsteps, a woman singing.
- A treasure map.
- 1. c.; 2. b.; 3. c.

Seeing the elephant

- `A`wa`y: Helps you, A Native American Indian; Uwe Dresler: From Nuremberg, Once lived in Brooklyn, NYC, A photographer.
- An edelweiss flower,
- 1. c.; 2. a.; 3. c.

A time tunnel
- True: AD's home is in Los Gatos.
- `A`wa`y (Mona)
- a. <u>too</u> = two, <u>to</u> = 22;
  b. be<u>fore</u> = four = 84, <u>to</u> = two; c. forgo<u>tten</u> = ten;
  d. <u>ate</u> = eight; e. <u>tent</u> = ten; ba<u>sics</u> = 6; <u>for</u> = four = 164

Sleepyhead
- Real names for flowers: oracle oak, California coffeeberry; wild cucumber.
- The leaves and berries of a toyon plant.
- 1. c.; 2. b.; 3. c.

Fishhooks
- True: He came to California from Mexico with some of his family.; He was the most wanted man in California.; He was a hero for some people.
- A primitive fishhook.
- 1. c.; 2. a.; 3. c.

For want of a nail …
- The thirteen colonies that declared independence from Great Britain, in 1776.
- An embroidery hoop
- "For want of a nail, the shoe was lost. For want of a shoe, the horse was lost. For want of a horse, the rider was lost. For want of a rider, the battle was lost. For want of a battle, the kingdom was lost. And all for the want of a horseshoe nail."

Shot like a dog, by a dog
- I love you.
- Dice.
- True: b.; d.; e.